THE SUPER EASY MEDITERRANEAN DIET COOKBOOK FOR BEGINNERS:

250 quick and scrumptious recipes WITH 5 OR LESS INGREDIENTS | 2-WEEK MEAL PLAN INCLUDED

By

Wilda Buckley

© **Copyright 2020 – Wilda Buckley - All rights reserved.**

The content contained within this book may not be reproduced, duplicated or transmitted without direct written permission from the author or the publisher.

Under no circumstances will any blame or legal responsibility be held against the publisher, or author, for any damages, reparation, or monetary loss due to the information contained within this book. Either directly or indirectly.

Legal Notice:

This book is copyright protected. This book is only for personal use. You cannot amend, distribute, sell, use, quote or paraphrase any part, or the content within this book, without the consent of the author or publisher.

Disclaimer Notice:

Please note the information contained within this document is for educational and entertainment purposes only. All effort has been executed to present accurate, up to date, and reliable, complete information. No warranties of any kind are declared or implied. Readers acknowledge that the author is not engaging in the rendering of legal, financial, medical or professional advice. The content within this book has been derived from various sources. Please consult a licensed professional before attempting any techniques outlined in this book.

By reading this document, the reader agrees that under no circumstances is the author responsible for any losses, direct or indirect, which are incurred as a result of the use of information contained within this document, including, but not limited to, — errors, omissions, or inaccuracies.

TABLE OF CONTENTS

INTRODUCTION		6
APPETIZER AND SNACK RECIPES		7
1.	Light & Creamy Garlic Hummus	7
2.	Perfect Queso	7
3.	Creamy Potato Spread	7
4.	Creamy Artichoke Dip	8
5.	Flavorful Roasted Baby Potatoes	8
6.	Perfect Italian Potatoes	8
7.	Garlic Pinto Bean Dip	8
8.	Creamy Eggplant Dip	9
9.	Jalapeno Chickpea Hummus	9
10.	Creamy Pepper Spread	9
11.	Healthy Spinach Dip	9
12.	Spicy Chicken Dip	10
13.	Raisins Cinnamon Peaches	10
14.	Lemon Pear Compote	10
15.	Strawberry Stew	10
16.	Brussels Sprouts and Pistachios	11
17.	Spiced Up Kale Chips	11
18.	Crazy Almond Crackers	11
19.	Superb Stuffed Mushrooms	12
20.	Flax and Almond Crunchies	12
21.	Mashed Up Celeriac	12
22.	Easy Medi Kale	12
23.	Black Bean Hummus	13
24.	Full Eggs in a Squash	13
25.	Simple Coconut Porridge	13
26.	Authentic Yogurt and Cucumber Salad	13
27.	Almond and Chocolate Butter Dip	14
28.	Cherry and Olive Bites	14
29.	Mouthwatering Panna Cotta with Mixed Berry Compote	14
30.	Lemon Mousse	14
31.	Minty Watermelon Salad	15
32.	Mascarpone and Fig Crostini	15
33.	Crunchy Sesame Cookies	15
34.	Creamy Rice Pudding	15
35.	Ricotta-Lemon Cheesecake	16
36.	Thyme Zucchini Chips	16
37.	Collagen Protein Bars	16
38.	Oven-Fried Chicken Nuggets	17
39.	Tropical Pineapple Smoothie	17
40.	Strawberry Coconut Parfait	17
41.	Smoked Salmon with Avocado	17
42.	Open-Face Sandwich	18
43.	Cilantro Lime Shrimp and Avocado Salad	18
44.	Pizza Margherita	18
45.	Fajitas	18
BREAKFAST RECIPES		19
46.	Eggs with Zucchini Noodles	19
47.	Banana Oats	19
48.	Berry Oats	19
49.	Sun-dried Tomatoes Oatmeal	19
50.	Quinoa Muffins	20
51.	Watermelon "Pizza"	20
52.	Cheesy Yogurt	20
53.	Cauliflower Fritters	20
54.	Corn and Shrimp Salad	21
55.	Walnuts Yogurt Mix	21
56.	Tahini Pine Nuts Toast	21
57.	Blueberries Quinoa	21
58.	Raspberries and Yogurt Smoothie	22
59.	Cottage Cheese and Berries Omelet	22
60.	Salmon Frittata	22
61.	Avocado and Olive Paste on Toasted Rye Bread	22
62.	Avocado and Chickpea Sandwiches	23

63.	Raisin Quinoa Breakfast	23
64.	Banana Cinnamon Fritters	23
65.	Veggie Casserole	23
66.	Ground Beef and Brussels Sprouts	24
67.	Italian Mini Meatballs	24
68.	Mushroom and Olives Steaks	24
69.	Salmon Kebabs	24
70.	Mediterranean Baked Salmon	25
71.	Feta Cheese Baked in Foil	25
72.	Avocado, Roasted Mushroom and Feta Spaghetti	25
73.	Tomato, Arugula and Feta Spaghetti	25
74.	Zucchini Fritters	26
75.	Cheesy Cauliflower Florets	26

MAIN DISH RECIPES 27

76.	Steak with Olives and Mushrooms	27
77.	Spicy Mustard Chicken	27
78.	Walnut and Oregano Crusted Chicken	27
79.	Chicken and Onion Casserole	27
80.	Chicken and Mushrooms	28
81.	Blue Cheese and Mushroom Chicken	28
82.	Herb-Roasted Lamb Leg	28
83.	Spring Lamb Stew	28
84.	Balsamic Roasted Carrots and Baby Onions	29
85.	Baked Cauliflower	29
86.	Baked Bean and Rice Casserole	29
87.	Okra and Tomato Casserole	29
88.	Spicy Baked Feta with Tomatoes	30
89.	Baked Lemon-Butter Fish	30
90.	Fish Taco Bowl	30
91.	Scallops with Creamy Bacon Sauce	30
92.	Shrimp and Avocado Lettuce Cups	31
93.	Garlic Butter Shrimp	31
94.	Parmesan-Garlic Salmon with Asparagus	31
95.	Seared-Salmon Shirataki Rice Bowls	32
96.	Pork Rind Salmon Cakes	32
97.	Creamy Dill Salmon	33
98.	Chicken-Basil Alfredo with Shirataki Noodles	33
99.	Chicken Quesadilla	33
100.	Garlic-Parmesan Chicken Wings	34
101.	Chicken Skewers with Peanut Sauce	34
102.	Braised Chicken Thighs with Kalamata Olives	34
103.	Buttery Garlic Chicken	35
104.	Heart-Warming Medi Tilapia	35
105.	Pistachio Sole Fish	35
106.	Exquisite Sardines and Raisin Croquettes	36
107.	Grilled Chicken with Lemon and Fennel	36
108.	Hearty Pork Belly Casserole	36
109.	Healthy Mediterranean Lamb Chops	36
110.	Amazingly Baked Chicken Breast	37
111.	Homely Tuscan Tuna Salad	37
112.	Cool Garbanzo and Spinach Beans	37
113.	Clean Eating Medi Stuffed Chicken Breasts	38
114.	Lemony Garlic Shrimp	38
115.	Completely Herbed Up Feisty Baby Potatoes	38
116.	Mediterranean Kale Dish	39
117.	Yogurt Marinated Tenderloin	39
118.	Buttery Herb Lamb Chops	39

SIDE RECIPES 40

119.	Lemon Fruit and Nut Bars	40
120.	Cauliflower Fried Rice with Bacon	40
121.	Halloumi Cheese with Butter-Fried Eggplant	40
122.	White Lasagna Stuffed Peppers	40
123.	Boiled Eggs with Butter and Thyme	41
124.	Fluffy Microwave Scrambled Eggs	41
125.	Caesar Salad Deviled Eggs	41
126.	Caesar Egg Salad Lettuce Wraps	42
127.	Sour Cream and Chive Egg Clouds	42

#	Recipe	Page
128.	Turkey and Cheese Rolls	42
129.	Bacon-Wrapped Avocado Fries	42
130.	Crispy Sweet Potato Fries	43
131.	Baked Eggs and Asparagus with Parmesan	43
132.	Cauliflower-Spinach Side Dish	43
133.	Savory Salmon Fat Bombs	43
134.	Pistachio Arugula Salad	44
135.	Potato Salad	44
136.	Flavorful Braised Kale	44
137.	Bean Salad	45
138.	Basil Tomato Skewers	45
139.	Olives with Feta	45
140.	Black Bean Medley	45
141.	Grilled Fish with Lemons	45
142.	Lemon Faro Bowl	46
143.	Chickpea & Red Pepper Delight	46
144.	Pesto Pasta	46
145.	Eggplant Rolls	47
146.	Heavenly Quinoa	47
147.	Roasted Squash Bisque	47
148.	Red Egg Skillet	47

SOUP AND STEWS RECIPES — 48

#	Recipe	Page
149.	Meatball Soup	48
150.	Soup with Eggs	48
151.	Peas Soup	48
152.	Red Lentil Soup	48
153.	Gazpacho	49
154.	Melon Gazpacho	49
155.	Chicken Soup	49
156.	Spicy Tomato Soup	49
157.	Chicken Strips Soup	49
158.	Tomato Bean Soup	50
159.	Zucchini Soup	50
160.	Pasta Soup	50
161.	White Mushrooms Soup	50
162.	Lamb Soup	50
163.	Lemon Zest Soup	51
164.	Pumpkin Soup	51
165.	Lentil Soup	51
166.	Chickpea Soup	51
167.	Chicken & Tomato Soup	52
168.	Chicken & Quinoa Stew	52
169.	Vegetable & Lentil Soup	52
170.	Carrot Soup	53
171.	Lentil & Spinach Soup	53
172.	Greek Veggie Soup	53
173.	Veggie Stew	54
174.	Carrot & Mushroom Soup	54
175.	White Bean & Swiss Chard Stew	54
176.	White Bean & Kale Soup	54
177.	Bacon & Potato Soup	54
178.	Lemon Chicken Soup	55

VEGETARIAN RECIPES — 56

#	Recipe	Page
179.	Mediterranean Veggie Bowl	56
180.	Grilled Veggie and Hummus Wrap	56
181.	Spanish Green Beans	56
182.	Rustic Cauliflower and Carrot Hash	57
183.	Roasted Cauliflower and Tomatoes	57
184.	Roasted Acorn Squash	57
185.	Sautéed Garlic Spinach	58
186.	Garlicky Sautéed Zucchini with Mint	58
187.	Stewed Okra	58
188.	Sweet Veggie-Stuffed Peppers	58
189.	Vegetable-Stuffed Grape Leaves	59
190.	Grilled Eggplant Rolls	59
191.	Crispy Zucchini Fritters	59
192.	Cheesy Spinach Pies	60
193.	Instant Pot Black Eyed Peas	60
194.	Green Beans and Potatoes in Olive Oil	60
195.	Nutritious Vegan Cabbage	61
196.	Instant Pot Horta and Potatoes	61
197.	Instant Pot Jackfruit Curry	61

198.	Instant Pot Collard Greens with Tomatoes	61
199.	Instant Pot Artichokes with Mediterranean Aioli	62
200.	Instant Pot Millet Pilaf	62
201.	Instant Pot Stuffed Sweet Potatoes	62
202.	Instant Pot Couscous and Vegetable Medley	63

DESSERT RECIPES — 64

203.	Chocolate Ganache	64
204.	Chocolate Covered Strawberries	64
205.	Strawberry Angel Food Dessert	64
206.	Key Lime Pie	64
207.	Ice Cream Sandwich Dessert	65
208.	Bananas Foster	65
209.	Rhubarb Strawberry Crunch	65
210.	Frosty Strawberry Dessert	65
211.	Dessert Pie	66
212.	Sugar-Coated Pecans	66
213.	Jalapeño Popper Spread	66
214.	Brown Sugar Smokies	67
215.	Fruit Dip	67
216.	Banana & Tortilla Snacks	67
217.	Caramel Popcorn	67
218.	Apple and Berries Ambrosia	67
219.	Chocolate, Almond, and Cherry Clusters	68
220.	Chocolate and Avocado Mousse	68
221.	Coconut Blueberries with Brown Rice	68
222.	Glazed Pears with Hazelnuts	68
223.	Lemony Blackberry Granita	69
224.	Lemony Tea and Chia Pudding	69
225.	Mint Banana Chocolate Sorbet	69
226.	Raspberry Yogurt Basted Cantaloupe	69
227.	Simple Apple Compote	70
228.	Simple Peanut Butter and Chocolate Balls	70
229.	Simple Spiced Sweet Pecans	70
230.	Overnight Oats with Raspberries	70
231.	Yogurt Sundae	71
232.	Blackberry-Yogurt Green	71
233.	Moroccan Stuffed Dates	71
234.	Almond Cookies	71
235.	Watermelon Cream	72
236.	Grapes Stew	72
237.	Cocoa Sweet Cherry Cream	72
238.	Spanish Nougat	72
239.	Cinnamon Butter Cookies	73
240.	Best French Meringues	73
241.	Cinnamon Palmiers	73
242.	Baked Apples	73
243.	Pumpkin Baked with Dry Fruit	74
244.	Quick Peach Tarts	74
245.	Bulgarian Rice Pudding	74
246.	Caramel Cream	74
247.	Yogurt-Strawberries Ice Pops	75
248.	Fresh Strawberries in Mascarpone and Rose Water	75
249.	Delicious French Eclairs	75
250.	Blueberry Yogurt Dessert	75

WEEK 1 MEAL PLAN — 77
WEEK 2 MEAL PLAN — 77
CONCLUSION — 78

INTRODUCTION

The Mediterranean diet is straightforward, easy to follow, and delicious; your transition to this diet will be a lot easier and smoother if you do a little bit of preparation beforehand.

You must have the right ingredients on hand, know about some of the foods you'll be eating, and have an idea of the meals you'd like to prepare. You'll also want to gradually (or immediately, if you're eager) rid the house of the foods that you'll no longer be eating.

While there are no supplements or specially packaged foods to buy, there are several key ingredients that you'll need to stock up on, and you'll also want to locate sources for the freshest and most healthful fruits, vegetables, and fish.

Preparing for the Mediterranean diet is largely about preparing yourself for a new way of eating, adjusting your attitude toward food into one of joyful expectation and appreciation of good meals and good company. It's like a mindset as anything else, so you'll want to make your environment one in which the Mediterranean way of eating can be naturally followed and easily enjoyed.

Preparing for the Mediterranean diet can be as simple as getting out the good dishes so that you can fully enjoy your meals or visiting a few local markets to check out the freshness and prices of their offerings.

You can take a month to prepare your pantry and yourself, or you can take just a few days, but a little time spent in advance can make all the difference in those first few weeks of your healthful new lifestyle.

You don't need to go out and buy special appliances, hard-to-find or expensive ingredients, special supplements, or even new workout gear on the Mediterranean diet. Still, a few things will make your transition to the diet easier and more fun.

Before starting the diet, it would be helpful to spend a week or two cutting back on the least healthy foods you are currently eating. You might start with fast food if you frequent the drive-through or eliminate cream-based sauces and soups. You can then start cutting back on processed foods like chips, boxed dinners, and frozen meals.

Some other things to start trimming might be sodas, coffee with a lot of milk and sugar, butter, and red meats such as beef, pork, and lamb. You don't have to eliminate these things during this period, but you'd be surprised at how quickly your body adjusts if you gradually wean yourself from them. It can make it much easier to adapt to the diet once you do begin in earnest.

The Mediterranean diet isn't just a way to eat; it's a way to love eating. Don't just engage in the diet, consider trying out their culture as well; where seasonal and fresh ingredients are cherished, dishes are generously shared and simply prepared, and lastly, time is very well-spent by lingering over a conversation, food, and wine.

Having the lifestyle in the Mediterranean way can not only improve your health and help you lose weight, but it can also encourage you to slow down, at least two or three times a day, and take a break from a hectic schedule and a busy life.

Have fun discovering the Mediterranean diet; consider spending weekends at your local farmers' market and have an adventure trying out various ingredients. Have more quality time with your family and friends by simply sharing your delicious meals.

The Mediterranean diet isn't just about having a healthy life; it's about having great pleasure and happiness!

APPETIZER AND SNACK RECIPES

1. Light & Creamy Garlic Hummus

Preparation Time: 10 minutes
Cooking Time: 40 minutes
Servings: 12

Ingredients
- 1 1/2 cups dry chickpeas, rinsed
- 2 1/2 tbsp. fresh lemon juice
- 1 tbsp. garlic, minced
- 1/2 cup tahini
- 6 cups of water

Directions
1. Add water and chickpeas into the instant pot.
2. Seal pot with a lid and select manual and set timer for 40 minutes.
3. Once done, allow to release pressure naturally. Remove lid.
4. Drain chickpeas well and reserved 1/2 cup chickpeas liquid.
5. Transfer chickpeas, reserved liquid, lemon juice, garlic, tahini, pepper, and salt into the food processor and process until smooth.
6. Serve and enjoy.

Nutrition: 152 Calories 6.9g Fat 17g Carbohydrates

2. Perfect Queso

Preparation Time: 10 minutes
Cooking Time: 15 minutes
Servings: 16

Ingredients
- 1 lb. ground beef
- 32 oz. Velveeta cheese, cut into cubes
- 10 oz. can tomato, diced
- 1 1/2 tbsp. taco seasoning
- 1 tsp chili powder

Directions
1. Set instant pot on sauté mode.
2. Add meat, 1 onion, taco seasoning, chili powder, pepper, and salt into the pot and cook until meat is no longer pink.
3. Add tomatoes and stir well. Top with cheese and do not stir.
4. Seal pot with lid and cook on high for 4 minutes.
5. Once done, release pressure using quick release. Remove lid.
6. Stir everything well and serve.

Nutrition: 257 Calories 15.9g Fat 10.2g Carbohydrates

3. Creamy Potato Spread

Preparation Time: 10 minutes
Cooking Time: 15 minutes
Servings: 6

Ingredients
- 1 lb. sweet potatoes, peeled and chopped
- 3/4 tbsp. fresh chives, chopped
- 1/2 tsp paprika
- 1 tbsp. garlic, minced
- 1 cup tomato puree

Directions
1. Add all ingredients except chives into the inner pot of instant pot and stir well.
2. Seal pot with lid and cook on high for 15 minutes.
3. When done, release pressure naturally for 10 minutes then releases remaining using quick release. Remove lid.
4. Transfer instant pot sweet potato mixture into the food processor and process until smooth.
5. Garnish with chives and serve.

Nutrition: 108 Calories 0.3g Fat 25.4g Carbohydrates

5. Creamy Artichoke Dip

Preparation Time: 10 minutes
Cooking Time: 5 minutes
Servings: 8

Ingredients
- 28 oz. can artichoke hearts, drain and quartered
- 1 1/2 cups parmesan cheese, shredded
- 1 cup sour cream, mayonnaise
- 3.5 oz. can green chilies
- 1 cup of water

Directions
1. Add artichokes, water, and green chilies into the instant pot.
2. Seal pot with the lid and select manual and set timer for 1 minute.
3. Once done, release pressure using quick release. Remove lid. Drain excess water.
4. Set instant pot on sauté mode. Cook the remaining ingredients and stir well until cheese is melted.
5. Serve and enjoy.

Nutrition: 262 Calories 7.6g Fat 14.4g Carbohydrates

6. Flavorful Roasted Baby Potatoes

Preparation Time: 10 minutes
Cooking Time: 10 minutes
Servings: 4

Ingredients
- 2 lbs. baby potatoes, clean and cut in half
- 1/2 cup vegetable stock
- 3/4 tsp garlic powder
- 1 tsp onion powder, paprika
- 2 tsp Italian seasoning

Directions
1. Pour oil into the inner pot of instant pot and set the pot on sauté mode.
2. Add potatoes and sauté for 5 minutes. Add remaining ingredients and stir well.
3. Seal pot with lid and cook on high for 5 minutes.
4. Once done, release pressure using quick release. Remove lid.
5. Stir well and serve.

Nutrition: 175 Calories 4.5g Fat 29.3g Carbohydrates

7. Perfect Italian Potatoes

Preparation Time: 10 minutes
Cooking Time: 7 minutes
Servings: 6

Ingredients
- 2 lbs. baby potatoes, clean and cut in half
- 3/4 cup vegetable broth
- 6 oz. Italian dry dressing mix

Direction
1. Incorporate all ingredients into the inner pot of instant pot and stir well.
2. Seal pot with lid and cook on high for 7 minutes.
3. Once done, allow to release pressure naturally for 3 minutes then release remaining using quick release. Remove lid.
4. Stir well and serve.

Nutrition: 149 Calories 0.3g Fat 41.6g Carbohydrates

8. Garlic Pinto Bean Dip

Preparation Time: 10 minutes
Cooking Time: 43 minutes
Servings: 6

Ingredients
- 1 cup dry pinto beans, rinsed
- 1/2 tsp cumin
- 1/2 cup salsa
- 2 chipotle peppers in adobo sauce
- 5 cups vegetable stock

Directions
1. Add beans, stock, 2 garlic cloves, and chipotle peppers into the instant pot.
2. Seal pot with lid and cook on high for 43 minutes.
3. Once done, release pressure using quick release. Remove lid.
4. Drain beans well and reserve 1/2 cup of stock.
5. Transfer beans, reserve stock, and remaining ingredients into the food processor and process until smooth.
6. Serve and enjoy.

Nutrition: 129 Calories 0.9g Fat 23g Carbohydrates

10. Creamy Eggplant Dip

Preparation Time: 10 minutes
Cooking Time: 20 minutes
Servings: 4

Ingredients
- 1 eggplant
- 1/2 tsp paprika
- 1 tbsp. fresh lime juice
- 2 tbsp. tahini
- 1 garlic clove

Directions
1. Add 1 cup of water and eggplant into the instant pot.
2. Seal pot with the lid and select manual and set timer for 20 minutes.
3. Once done, release pressure using quick release. Remove lid.
4. Drain eggplant and let it cool.
5. Once the eggplant is cool then remove eggplant skin and transfer eggplant flesh into the food processor.
6. Pulse the remaining ingredients with food processor and process until smooth.
7. Serve and enjoy.

Nutrition: 108 Calories 7.8g Fat 9.7g Carbohydrates

11. Jalapeno Chickpea Hummus

Preparation Time: 10 minutes
Cooking Time: 25 minutes
Servings: 4

Ingredients
- 1 cup dry chickpeas, soaked overnight and drained
- 1 tsp ground cumin
- 1/4 cup jalapenos, diced
- 1/2 cup fresh cilantro
- 1 tbsp. tahini

Directions
1. Add chickpeas into the instant pot and cover with vegetable stock.
2. Seal pot with lid and cook on high for 25 minutes.
3. Once done, allow to release pressure naturally. Remove lid.
4. Drain chickpeas well and transfer into the food processor along with remaining ingredients and process until smooth.
5. Serve and enjoy.

Nutrition: 425 Calories 30.4g Fat 31.8g Carbohydrates

12. Creamy Pepper Spread

Preparation Time: 10 minutes
Cooking Time: 15 minutes
Servings: 4

Ingredients
- 1 lb. red bell peppers, chopped and remove seeds
- 1 1/2 tbsp. fresh basil
- 1 tbsp. olive oil
- 1 tbsp. fresh lime juice
- 1 tsp garlic, minced

Direction
1. Situate all ingredients into the inner pot of instant pot and stir well.
2. Seal pot with lid and cook on high for 15 minutes.
3. Once finish, let the pressure release naturally for 10 minutes then release the rest using quick release. Remove lid.
4. Transfer bell pepper mixture into the food processor and process until smooth.
5. Serve and enjoy.

Nutrition: 41 Calories 3.6g Fat 3.5g Carbohydrates

13. Healthy Spinach Dip

Preparation Time: 10 minutes
Cooking Time: 8 minutes
Servings: 4

Ingredients
- 14 oz. spinach
- 2 tbsp. fresh lime juice
- 1 tbsp. garlic, minced
- 2 tbsp. olive oil
- 2 tbsp. coconut cream

Directions
1. Add all ingredients except coconut cream into the instant pot and stir well.

2. Seal pot with lid and cook on low pressure for 8 minutes.
3. Once done, allow to release pressure naturally for 5 minutes then release remaining using quick release. Remove lid.
4. Add coconut cream and stir well and blend spinach mixture using a blender until smooth.
5. Serve and enjoy.

Nutrition: 109 Calories 9.2g Fat 6.6g Carbohydrates

14. Spicy Chicken Dip

Preparation Time: 10 minutes
Cooking Time: 15 minutes
Servings: 10

Ingredients
- 1 lb. chicken breast, skinless and boneless
- 1/2 cup sour cream
- 8 oz. cheddar cheese, cream cheese
- 1/2 cup chicken stock
- 2 jalapeno pepper, sliced

Directions
1. Add chicken, stock, jalapenos, and cream cheese into the instant pot.
2. Seal pot with lid and cook on high for 12 minutes.
3. Once done, release pressure using quick release. Remove lid.
4. Shred chicken using a fork.
5. Set pot on sauté. Put the rest of ingredients and continue cooking.
6. Serve and enjoy.

Nutrition: 248 Calories 19g Fat 1.6g Carbohydrates

15. Raisins Cinnamon Peaches

Preparation Time: 10 minutes
Cooking Time: 15 minutes
Servings: 4

Ingredients
- 4 peaches, cored and cut into chunks
- 1 tsp vanilla
- 1 tsp cinnamon
- 1/2 cup raisins
- 1 cup of water

Direction
1. Mix all ingredients into the inner pot of instant pot and stir well.
2. Seal pot with lid and cook on high for 15 minutes.
3. Once cooked, release pressure naturally for 10 minutes then releases the rest by quick release. Remove lid.
4. Stir and serve.

Nutrition: 118 Calories 0.5g Fat 29g Carbohydrates

16. Lemon Pear Compote

Preparation Time: 10 minutes
Cooking Time: 15 minutes
Servings: 6

Ingredients
- 3 cups pears, cored and cut into chunks
- 1 tsp vanilla
- 1 tsp liquid stevia
- 1 tbsp. lemon zest, grated
- 2 tbsp. lemon juice

Direction
1. Situate all ingredients into the inner pot of instant pot and stir well.
2. Seal pot with lid and cook on high for 15 minutes.
3. When cooked, let the pressure naturally release for 10 minutes then release remaining using quick release. Open it.
4. Stir and serve.

Nutrition: 50 Calories 0.2g Fat 12.7g Carbohydrates

17. Strawberry Stew

Preparation Time: 10 minutes
Cooking Time: 15 minutes
Servings: 4

Ingredients
- 12 oz. fresh strawberries, sliced
- 1 tsp vanilla
- 1 1/2 cups water
- 1 tsp liquid stevia
- 2 tbsp. lime juice

Direction
1. Mix all ingredients into the inner pot of instant pot and stir well.
2. Seal pot with lid and cook on high for 15 minutes.

3. Once cooked, allow to release pressure naturally for 10 minutes then by using quick release, let the remaining pressure out. Remove lid.
4. Stir and serve.

Nutrition: 36 Calories 0.3g Fat 8.5g Carbohydrates

18. **Brussels Sprouts and Pistachios**

Preparation Time: 15 minutes
Cooking Time: 15 minutes
Serving: 4

Ingredients
- 1-pound Brussels sprouts, trimmed and halved lengthwise
- 4 shallots, peeled and quartered
- 1 tablespoon extra-virgin olive oil
- ½ cup roasted pistachios, chopped
- ½ lemon juice and zest

Direction
1. Pre-heat your oven to 400 degrees Fahrenheit.
2. Wrap baking sheet with aluminum foil and keep aside.
3. Take a large bowl and add Brussels sprouts, shallots with olive oil and coat well.
4. Season sea salt, pepper, spread veggies evenly on sheet.
5. Bake for 15 minutes until lightly caramelized.
6. Remove oven and transfer to a serving bowl.
7. Toss with lemon zest, pistachios, lemon juice.
8. Serve warm and enjoy!

Nutrition: 126 Calories 7g Fat 6g Protein

19. **Spiced Up Kale Chips**

Preparation Time: 10 minutes
Cooking Time: 25 minutes
Serving: 4

Ingredients
- 3 cups kale, stemmed and thoroughly washed, torn into 2-inch pieces
- 1 tablespoon extra-virgin olive oil
- ½ teaspoon chili powder
- ¼ teaspoon sea salt

Direction
1. Pre-heat your oven to 300 degrees Fahrenheit.
2. Cover 2 baking sheets using parchment paper and keep aside.
3. Dry kale entirely and transfer to a large bowl.
4. Add olive oil and toss.
5. Make sure each leaf is covered.
6. Season kale with chili powder and salt, toss again.
7. Divide kale between baking sheets and spread into a single layer.
8. Bake for 25 minutes.
9. Cool the chips for 5 minutes and serve.
10. Enjoy!

Nutrition: 56 Calories 4g Fat 2g Protein

20. **Crazy Almond Crackers**

Preparation Time: 10 minutes
Cooking Time: 20 minutes
Serving: 20

Ingredients
- 1 cup almond flour
- ¼ teaspoon baking soda
- 3 tablespoons sesame seeds
- 1 egg, beaten

Direction
1. Pre-heat your oven to 350 degrees Fahrenheit.
2. Put two baking sheets with parchment paper and keep aside.
3. Mix the dry ingredients to a large bowl and add egg, mix well and form dough.
4. Divide dough into two balls.
5. Roll out the dough between two pieces of parchment paper.
6. Cut into crackers and transfer them to prepared baking sheet.
7. Bake for 15-20 minutes.
8. Do it in all the dough.
9. Leave crackers to cool and serve.

Nutrition: 302 Calories 28g Fat 9g Protein

21. Superb Stuffed Mushrooms

Preparation Time: 10 minutes
Cooking Time: 15 minutes
Serving: 4

Ingredients
- 4 Portobello mushrooms
- 1 cup crumbled blue cheese
- 2 teaspoons extra virgin olive oil
- Salt, to taste
- Fresh thyme

Directions
1. Preheat your oven to 350-degree Fahrenheit.
2. Cut out the stems from the mushrooms.
3. Chop them into small pieces.
4. Take a bowl and mix stem pieces with thyme, salt and blue cheese and mix well.
5. Fill up mushroom with the prepared cheese.
6. Top with some oil.
7. Take a baking sheet and place the mushrooms.
8. Bake for 15 minutes to 20 minutes.
9. Serve warm and enjoy!

Nutrition: 124 Calories 22.4g Fat 1.2g Protein

22. Flax and Almond Crunchies

Preparation Time: 15 minutes
Cooking Time: 60 minutes
Serving: 10

Ingredients
- ½ cup ground flax seeds
- ½ cup almond flour
- 1 tablespoon coconut flour
- 2 tablespoons shelled hemp seeds
- 2 tablespoons unsalted butter, melted

Direction
1. Pre-heat your oven to 300 degrees Fahrenheit.
2. Prep baking sheet using parchment paper, keep the prepared sheet on the side.
3. Add flax, coconut flour, almond, salt, hemp seed to a bowl and mix well.
4. Add 1 egg white and melted butter, mix well.
5. Transfer dough to sheet of parchment paper and cover with another sheet of paper.
6. Roll out dough.
7. Cut into crackers and bake for 60 minutes.
8. Cool and serve!

Nutrition: 47 Calories 6g Fat 0.2g Protein

23. Mashed Up Celeriac

Preparation Time: 10 minutes
Cooking Time: 20 minutes
Serving: 4

Ingredients
- 2 celeriac, washed, peeled and diced
- 2 teaspoons extra-virgin olive oil
- 1 tablespoon honey
- ½ teaspoon ground nutmeg

Direction
1. Pre-heat your oven to 400 degrees Fahrenheit.
2. Prepare the baking sheet with foil and keep it aside.
3. Take a large bowl and toss celeriac and olive oil.
4. Spread celeriac evenly on baking sheet.
5. Roast for 20 minutes until tender.
6. Transfer to large bowl.
7. Add honey and nutmeg.
8. Use a potato masher to mash the mixture until fluffy.
9. Season with salt and pepper.
10. Serve and enjoy!

Nutrition: 136 Calories 3g Fat 4g Protein

24. Easy Medi Kale

Preparation Time: 15 minutes
Cooking Time: 10 minutes
Serving: 6

Ingredients
- 12 cups kale, chopped
- 2 tablespoons lemon juice
- 1 tablespoon olive oil
- 1 tablespoon garlic, minced
- 1 teaspoon soy sauce

Direction
1. Add a steamer insert to your saucepan.
2. Pour water in the saucepan up to the bottom of the steamer.
3. Cover and bring water to boil (medium-high heat).
4. Add kale to the insert and steam for 7-8 minutes.
5. Take a large bowl and add lemon juice, garlic, olive oil, salt, soy sauce and pepper.
6. Mix well and add the steamed kale to the bowl.
7. Toss and serve.

Nutrition: 350 Calories 17g Fat 11g Protein

25. Black Bean Hummus

Preparation Time: 25 minutes
Cooking Time: 0 minute
Serving: 4

Ingredients
- 1 cup of cooked black beans
- 1 minced garlic clove
- 2 tablespoons of lemon juice
- 1 tablespoon of white wine vinegar
- ½ teaspoon of ground cumin

Direction
1. Situate all the ingredients to your blender except ½ head of lettuce.
2. Process until everything is smooth.
3. Allow to sit for 15 minutes and serve with the iceberg lettuce.

Nutrition 81 Calories 4g Fat 4g Protein

26. Full Eggs in a Squash

Preparation Time: 10 minutes
Cooking Time: 20 minutes
Serving: 5

Ingredients
- 2 acorn squash
- 6 whole eggs
- 2 tablespoons extra virgin olive oil
- 5-6 pitted dates
- 8 walnut halves

Direction
1. Pre-heat your oven to 375 degrees Fahrenheit.
2. Slice squash crosswise and prepare 3 slices with holes.
3. While slicing the squash, make sure that each slice has a measurement of ¾ inch thickness.
4. Remove the seeds from the slices.
5. Get baking sheet and line it with parchment paper.
6. Transfer the slices to your baking sheet and season them with salt and pepper.
7. Bake in your oven for 20 minutes.
8. Chop the walnuts and dates on your cutting board.
9. Take the baking dish out of the oven and drizzle slices with olive oil.
10. Beat egg into each of the holes in the slices and season well.
11. Sprinkle the chopped walnuts on top.
12. Bake for 10 minutes more.
13. Garnish with parsley and add maple syrup.

Nutrition: 198 Calories 12g Fat 8g Protein

27. Simple Coconut Porridge

Preparation Time: 15 minutes
Cooking Time: 0 minute
Serving: 6

Ingredients
- Powdered erythritol as needed
- 1 ½ cups almond milk, unsweetened
- 2 tablespoons vanilla protein powder
- 3 tablespoons Golden Flaxseed meal
- 2 tablespoons coconut flour

Direction
1. Take a bowl and mix in flaxseed meal, protein powder, coconut flour and mix well.
2. Add mix to saucepan (placed over medium heat).
3. Add almond milk and stir, let the mixture thicken.
4. Add your desired amount of sweetener and serve.

Nutrition: 259 Calories 13g Fat 16g Protein

28. Authentic Yogurt and Cucumber Salad

Preparation Time: 10 minutes
Cooking Time: 0 minute
Serving: 4

Ingredients
- 5-6 small cucumbers, peeled and diced
- 1 (8 ounces) container plain Greek yogurt
- 2 garlic cloves, minced
- 1 tablespoon fresh mint, minced
- 1 teaspoon dried oregano

Direction
1. Take a large bowl and add cucumbers, garlic, yogurt, mint, and oregano.
2. Season with salt and pepper.
3. Refrigerate the salad for 1 hour and serve.

Nutrition: 74 Calories 0.7g Fat 2g Protein

29. Almond and Chocolate Butter Dip

Preparation Time: 15 minutes
Cooking Time: 10 minutes
Serving: 14

Ingredients

- 1 cup Plain Greek Yogurt
- ½ cup almond butter
- 1/3 cup chocolate hazelnut spread
- 1 tablespoon honey
- 1 teaspoon vanilla

Direction

1. Take a medium-sized bowl and add the first five listed ingredients.
2. With an immersion blender, blend well until you have a smooth dip.
3. Serve with your favorite sliced fruit.

Nutrition: 115 Calories 8g Fat 4g Protein

30. Cherry and Olive Bites

Preparation Time: 15 minutes
Cooking Time: 0 minute
Serving: 30

Ingredients

- 24 cherry tomatoes, halved
- 24 black olives, pitted
- 24 feta cheese cubes
- 24 toothpick/decorative skewers

Direction

1. Use a toothpick or skewer and thread feta cheese, black olives, and cherry tomato halves in that order.
2. Repeat until all the ingredients are used.
3. Arrange in a serving platter.

Nutrition: 57 Calories: 5g Fa2g Protein

31. Mouthwatering Panna Cotta with Mixed Berry Compote

Preparation Time: 5 minutes
Cooking Time: 10 minutes
Serving: 4

Ingredients

- 2 cups of freshly divided mixed berries
- 1 package of plain gelatin powder
- 1 cup of milk
- 1 2/3 cup of heavy cream
- ¾ cup of divided sugar

Direction

1. Puree 1 cup of raspberries into a food processor.
2. Take a small saucepan and transfer the puree to that saucepan.
3. Add about ¼ cup of sugar and the remaining raspberries.
4. Cook over medium heat for 10 minutes, making sure to stir from time to time.
5. Remove the heat after 10 minutes and let cool.
6. Cover and chill in your fridge.
7. Take another saucepan and combine your milk and gelatin and wait until the gelatin softens.
8. Simmer over medium heat and keep stirring frequently to fully dissolve the gelatin.
9. Stir in the heavy cream alongside the rest of the sugar and cook for another 3-5 minutes.
10. Pour the mixture into 4 ramekins.
11. Chill them for 8 hours or overnight.
12. Invert the mold and place on a serving plate.
13. Once the Panna Cotta comes out, top it with your berry compote.

Nutrition: 191 Calories 15g Fat 6g Carbohydrates

32. Lemon Mousse

Preparation Time: 10 minutes
Cooking Time: 10 minutes
Serving: 4

Ingredients

- 1 cup coconut cream
- 8 ounces cream cheese, soft
- ¼ cup fresh lemon juice
- 3 pinches salt
- 1 teaspoon lemon liquid stevia

Direction

1. Pre-heat your oven to 350 degrees Fahrenheit.
2. Grease a ramekin with butter.
3. Beat cream, cream cheese, fresh lemon juice, salt and lemon liquid stevia in a mixer.
4. Pour batter into ramekin.
5. Bake for 10 minutes, then transfer mouse to serving glass.
6. Let chill for 2 hours and serve.

Nutrition: 395 Calories 31g Fat 3g Carbohydrates

33. Minty Watermelon Salad

Preparation Time: 10 minutes
Cooking Time: 0 minute
Serving: 6
Ingredients:
- 1 medium watermelon
- 1 c. fresh blueberries
- 2 tbsp. fresh mint leaves
- 2 tbsp. lemon juice
- 1/3 c. honey

Direction:
1. Cut the watermelon into 1-inch cubes. Put them in a bowl.
2. Evenly distribute the blueberries over the watermelon.
3. Next, finely chop the mint leaves and put them into a separate bowl.
4. Add the lemon juice and honey to the mint and whisk together.
5. Drizzle the mint dressing over the watermelon and blueberries. Serve cold.

Nutrition: 296 calories 23g fat 3.3g fiber

34. Mascarpone and Fig Crostini

Preparation Time: 8 minutes
Cooking Time: 15 minutes
Serving: 6

Ingredients:
- 1 long French baguette
- 4 tbsp. (½ stick) salted butter, melted
- 1 (8 oz.) tub mascarpone cheese
- 1 (12 oz.) jar fig jam or preserves
- 1 tbsp. sugar

Direction
1. Preheat the oven to 350°F.
2. Portion the bread to ¼-inch-thick slices.
3. Arrange the sliced bread on a sheet and rub each slice with the melted butter and small amount of sugar.
4. Next, put the baking sheet into your oven and toast the bread for 5 to 7 minutes, just until it turns to golden brown.
5. Let the bread cool slightly. Then, spread about a teaspoon or so of the mascarpone cheese on each piece of bread.
6. Lastly, put a teaspoon or so of the jam on top. Serve immediately.

Nutrition: 281 calories 18g fat 4g fiber

35. Crunchy Sesame Cookies

Preparation Time: 7 minutes
Cooking Time: 15 minutes
Serving: 6
Ingredients:
- 1 c. sesame seeds, hulled
- 1 c. sugar
- 8 tbsp. (1 stick) salted butter, softened
- 2 eggs
- 1¼ c. flour

Direction:
1. Preheat the oven to 350°F firstly. Then, toast the sesame seeds on a baking sheet for 3 minutes. Set aside and let cool.
2. Mix the sugar and the butter using the mixer.
3. Put the eggs slowly until well-blended.
4. Add the flour and toasted sesame seeds and mix until well-blended.
5. Drop spoonful of cookie dough onto your baking sheet and form them into round balls, about 1-inch in diameter, similar to a walnut.
6. Put in the oven. Then, bake approximately for 5 to 7 minutes or until golden brown.
7. Let the cookies cool and enjoy.

Nutrition: 301 calories 19g fat 2g fiber

36. Creamy Rice Pudding

Preparation Time: 11 minutes
Cooking Time: 50 minutes
Serving: 6
Ingredients:
- 1¼ c. long-grain rice
- 5 c. whole milk
- 1 c. sugar
- 1 tbsp. rose water or orange blossom water
- 1 tsp. cinnamon

Direction:
1. First, rinse the rice under cold water for 30 seconds.
2. Put the rice, milk, and sugar in a large pot. Bring to a gentle boil while continually stirring.
3. Turn the heat down to low and let simmer for 40 to 45 minutes, stirring every 3 to 4 minutes so that the rice does not stick to the bottom of the pot.
4. Next, add the rose water at the end and simmer for 5 minutes.
5. Divide the pudding into 6 bowls. Sprinkle the top with cinnamon. Lastly, cool for at least 1 hour before serving. Store in the fridge.

Nutrition: 303 calories 21g fat 2g fiber

37. Ricotta-Lemon Cheesecake

Preparation Time: 14 minutes
Cooking Time: 1 hour
Serving: 8

Ingredients:
- 2 (8 oz.) packages full-fat cream cheese
- 1 (16 oz.) container full-fat ricotta cheese
- 1½ c. granulated sugar
- 1 tbsp. lemon zest
- 5 eggs

Direction
1. Preheat the oven to 350°F.
2. Next, using a mixer, blend together the cream cheese and ricotta cheese.
3. Blend in the sugar and lemon zest.
4. Blend in the eggs; drop in 1 egg at a time, blend for 10 seconds, and repeat.
5. Line a 9-inch spring form pan with a parchment paper and nonstick spray. Bind the lower part of the pan with foil. Pour the cheesecake batter into the pan.
6. To make a water bath, get a baking or roasting pan larger than the cheesecake pan. Fill the roasting pan about 1/3 of the way up with warm water. Put the cheesecake pan into the water bath. Situate the whole thing in the oven and let the cheesecake bake for 1 hour.
7. After baking is complete, remove the cheesecake pan from the water bath and remove the foil. Let the cheesecake cool approximately for 1 hour on the countertop. Lastly, put it in the fridge to cool for at least 3 hours before serving.

Nutrition: 311 calories 20g fat 6g fiber

38. Thyme Zucchini Chips

Preparation Time: 7 minutes
Cooking Time: 2 hours
Serving: 4

Ingredients:
- 4 zucchinis, thinly sliced
- ½ tsp. dried thyme or 2 tsp. chopped fresh thyme
- 2 tbsp. avocado oil, divided
- ½ tsp. pink Himalayan salt or sea salt
- ½ tsp. garlic powder

Direction:
1. Spread the zucchini slices on paper towels without overlapping. Place a large baking sheet on top of the paper towels to help press out any moisture. Let sit for 15 minutes.
2. Preheat the oven to 235°F. Then, line the same baking sheet with parchment paper. Brush 1 tablespoon avocado oil on the parchment.
3. Arrange the zucchini slices on the lined baking sheet in a single layer and brush the remaining 1 tablespoon of avocado oil on top of the slices. In a small bowl, scourge the salt, garlic powder, and thyme. Sprinkle on top of the zucchini slices.
4. Bake for 1½ to 2 hours, or until crisp and golden brown. Allow the chips to cool before enjoying.

Nutrition: 314 calories 24g fat 7g fiber

39. Collagen Protein Bars

Preparation Time: 12 minutes
Cooking Time: 30 minutes
Serving: 8

Ingredients:
- 1 c. dried dates, pitted
- 1 c. dried cranberries
- ½ c. collagen peptides powder
- ¼ tsp. pink Himalayan salt or sea salt
- 2 tsp. coconut oil

Direction:
1. First, line an 8-by-8-inch baking pan with parchment paper, leaving an overhang for easy lifting.
2. Combine the dates and cranberries in a blender or food processor and pulse until chopped completely. Add the collagen powder, salt, and coconut oil and pulse until fully combined.
3. Next, transfer the mixture to the lined baking pan and press it down into an even layer. Place the pan in your freezer for 20 minutes, or until firm.
4. Remove from the baking pan by lifting the parchment paper. Cut into 8 bars.

Nutrition: 297 calories 21g fat 5g fiber

40. Oven-Fried Chicken Nuggets

Preparation Time: 18 minutes
Cooking Time: 30 minutes
Serving: 4

Ingredients:
- ½ c. full-fat unsweetened coconut milk (store-bought or homemade, here)
- 1 tbsp. white wine vinegar
- ½ tsp. pink Himalayan salt or sea salt
- 1 lb. boneless, skinless chicken breasts, cut into 1½-inch pieces
- 1½ c. crushed plain pork rinds

Direction:
1. Preheat the oven to 400°F. Then, line your large baking sheet with parchment paper.
2. In a large baking pan, mix together the coconut milk, vinegar, and salt. Add the chicken pieces, then let sit for 10 minutes.
3. Pour the pork rinds into a shallow bowl. One at a time, remove the chicken pieces from your baking pan, let the excess coconut milk mixture drip off, and coat in the pork rinds, firmly pressing the crumbs onto the chicken.
4. Lastly, place on the lined baking sheet in a single layer and bake for 16 to 20 minutes approximately, or until crisp and golden brown. Serve hot.

Nutrition: 298 calories 20g fat 7g fiber

41. Tropical Pineapple Smoothie

Preparation Time: 5 minutes
Cooking Time: 0 minutes
Serving: 1

Ingredients:
- 1 c. pineapple chunks, frozen
- ½ banana
- ¼ c. mango chunks, frozen
- ½ c. orange juice
- ½ c. full-fat unsweetened coconut milk

Direction:
1. Combine the pineapple, banana, mango, orange juice, and coconut milk in a blender and process until smooth.
2. Pour into a glass and enjoy. Smoothies are best when you drink them right away.

Nutrition: 300 calories 18g fat 2g fiber

42. Strawberry Coconut Parfait

Preparation Time: 7 minutes
Cooking Time: 0 minutes
Serving: 1

Ingredients:
- 1 c. plain unsweetened coconut yogurt
- 1 tbsp. raw honey
- ½ tsp. vanilla powder
- 1 c. chopped strawberries
- ½ c. Granola

Direction:
1. First, in your small bowl, mix together the coconut yogurt, honey, and vanilla powder until combined.
2. In a large glass, spoon one-third of the yogurt mixture into the bottom, followed by one-third of the strawberries, then one-third of the granola. Repeat the same layers twice more.
3. Serve immediately.
4. If you're making extra parfaits, store the yogurt and the granola separately and put the parfait together right before serving, so the granola will not get soggy.

Nutrition: 281 calories 16g fat 1g fiber

43. Smoked Salmon with Avocado

Preparation Time: 11 minutes
Cooking Time: 5 minutes
Serving: 2

Ingredients:
- 1 avocado, pitted, peeled, and sliced
- 2 tbsp. AIP Mayo
- 8 oz. smoked salmon
- 1 tbsp. capers
- 1 tbsp. chopped fresh dill (optional)

Direction:
1. Divide the avocado slices between two medium plates, then add a dollop of mayo and half the salmon, capers, and dill (if using) to each plate.

Nutrition: 290 calories 21g fat 4g fiber

44. Open-Face Sandwich

Preparation Time: 8 minutes
Cooking Time: 25 minutes
Serving: 2

Ingredients:
- 6 slices bacon
- 2 tbsp. AIP Mayo
- 2 AIP Garlic Herb Flatbreads
- ½ c. arugula
- ½ avocado, peeled, pitted, and sliced

Direction:
1. First, in your large skillet, cook the bacon over medium heat for 10 to 12 minutes, or until it's crisp. Then, transfer to your plate lined with paper towels.
2. Lay out the flatbreads, and spread 1 tablespoon of mayo on each one. Divide the arugula between the flatbreads, and then top with 3 bacon slices. Arrange the avocado on top of the bacon.

Nutrition: 289 calories 18g fat 5g fiber

45. Cilantro Lime Shrimp and Avocado Salad

Preparation Time: 7 minutes
Cooking Time: 10 minutes
Serving: 1

Ingredients:
- 6 oz. shrimp, peeled and deveined
- 2 c. mixed greens
- 1 avocado, pitted, peeled, and diced
- 1 scallion, finely sliced
- ¼ c. Cilantro Lime Vinaigrette

Direction:
1. First, fill a small pot with filtered water and bring to a boil. Add the shrimp and cook for 2 or 3 minutes, until they turn pink and become opaque. Using a strainer, drain the shrimp and immediately rinse under cold running water until they're cool to touch.
2. Next, put the mixed greens in a salad bowl. Top with the avocado, scallions, and cooked shrimp.
3. Drizzle the dressing onto the salad, then toss to combine. Enjoy right away.

Nutrition: 298 calories 19g fat 2g fiber

46. Pizza Margherita

Preparation Time: 11 minutes
Cooking Time: 15 minutes
Serving: 4

Ingredients:
- 4 (6-inch) pizza crusts
- 4 tbsp. olive oil
- 8 oz. fresh mozzarella cheese, thinly sliced
- 2 ripe tomatoes, thinly sliced
- ½ c. thinly sliced fresh basil leaves

Direction:
1. Preheat the oven to 400°F. Place the pizza crusts onto a rimmed baking sheet.
2. Brush the crusts with the olive oil. Then, top with the mozzarella cheese and tomato slices.
3. Bake for 10 minutes, or until the mozzarella is melted and the tomatoes are wilted.
4. Top with the fresh basil leaves.

Nutrition: 303 calories 20g fat 3g fiber

47. Fajitas

Preparation Time: 12 minutes
Cooking Time: 3 hours
Serving: 4

Ingredients:
- 2 lb. steak, cut into strips (buy whatever is on sale)
- 2 bell peppers, sliced
- 1 medium onion, sliced
- 15 oz. salsa (you can also use spicy diced tomatoes)
- 2 tbsp. fajita seasoning

Direction:
1. Put the entire ingredients into your slow cooker. Then, cook on high for 3 hours or on low for 5–6 hours.
2. Serve with tortillas or over rice for a complete meal.

Nutrition: 298 calories 21g fat 1g fiber

BREAKFAST RECIPES

48. Eggs with Zucchini Noodles

Preparation Time: 10 minutes
Cooking Time: 11 minutes
Servings: 2

Ingredients:
- 2 tablespoons extra-virgin olive oil
- 3 zucchinis, cut with a spiralizer
- 4 eggs
- A pinch of red pepper flakes
- 1 tablespoon basil, chopped

Directions:
1. In a bowl, combine the zucchini noodles with salt, pepper and the olive oil and toss well.
2. Grease a baking sheet with cooking spray and divide the zucchini noodles into 4 nests on it.
3. Crack an egg on top of each nest, sprinkle salt, pepper and the pepper flakes on top and bake at 350 degrees F for 11 minutes.
4. Divide the mix between plates, sprinkle the basil on top and serve.

Nutrition: 296 calories 23g fat 3.3g fiber

49. Banana Oats

Preparation Time: 10 minutes
Cooking Time: 0 minutes
Servings: 2

Ingredients:
- ½ cup cold brewed coffee
- 2 dates, pitted
- 2 tablespoons cocoa powder
- 1 cup rolled oats
- 1 and ½ tablespoons chia seeds

Directions:
1. In a blender, combine the 1 banana with the ¾ almond milk and the rest of the ingredients, pulse, divide into bowls and serve for breakfast.

Nutrition: 451 calories 25g fat 9.9g fiber

50. Berry Oats

Preparation Time: 5 minutes
Cooking Time: 0 minute
Servings: 2

Ingredients:
- ½ cup rolled oats
- 1 cup almond milk
- ¼ cup chia seeds
- 2 teaspoons honey
- 1 cup berries, pureed

Directions:
1. In a bowl, combine the oats with the milk and the rest of the ingredients except 1 tbsp. of yogurt, toss, divide into bowls, top with the yogurt and serve cold for breakfast.

Nutrition: 420 calories 30g fat 6.4g protein

51. Sun-dried Tomatoes Oatmeal

Preparation Time: 10 minutes
Cooking Time: 25 minutes
Servings: 4

Ingredients:
- 3 cups water
- 1 cup almond milk
- 1 tablespoon olive oil
- 1 cup steel-cut oats
- ¼ cup sun-dried tomatoes, chopped

Directions:
1. In a pan, scourge water with the milk, bring to a boil over medium heat.
2. Meanwhile, pre-heat pan with the oil over medium-high heat, add the oats, cook them for about 2 minutes and transfer m to the pan with the milk.
3. Stir the oats, add the tomatoes and simmer over medium heat for 23 minutes.
4. Divide the mix into bowls, sprinkle the red pepper flakes on top and serve for breakfast.

Nutrition: 170 calories 17.8g fat 1.5g protein

52. Quinoa Muffins

Preparation Time: 10 minutes
Cooking Time: 30 minutes
Servings: 12

Ingredients:
- 6 eggs, whisked
- 1 cup Swiss cheese, grated
- 1 small yellow onion, chopped
- 1 cup quinoa, white mushrooms
- ½ cup sun-dried tomatoes, chopped

Directions:
1. In a bowl, combine the eggs with salt, pepper and the rest of the ingredients and whisk well.
2. Divide this into a silicone muffin pan, bake at 350 degrees F for 30 minutes and serve for breakfast.

Nutrition: 123 calories 5.6g fat 7.5g protein

53. Watermelon "Pizza"

Preparation Time: 10 minutes
Cooking Time: 0 minutes
Servings: 4

Ingredients:
- 1 watermelon slice cut 1-inch thick and then from the center cut into 4 wedges resembling pizza slices
- 6 Kalamata olives, pitted and sliced
- 1-ounce feta cheese, crumbled
- ½ tablespoon balsamic vinegar
- 1 teaspoon mint, chopped

Directions:
1. Arrange the watermelon "pizza" on a plate, sprinkle the olives and the rest of the ingredients on each slice and serve right away for breakfast.

Nutrition: 90 calories 3g fat 2g protein

54. Cheesy Yogurt

Preparation Time: 4 hours and 5 minutes
Cooking Time: 0 minutes
Servings: 4

Ingredients:
- 1 cup Greek yogurt
- 1 tablespoon honey
- ½ cup feta cheese, crumbled

Directions:
1. In a blender, combine the yogurt with the honey and the cheese and pulse well.
2. Divide into bowls and freeze for 4 hours before serving for breakfast.

Nutrition: 161 calories 10g fat 6.6g protein

55. Cauliflower Fritters

Preparation Time: 10 minutes
Cooking Time: 50 minutes
Servings: 4

Ingredients:
- 30 ounces canned chickpeas, drained and rinsed
- 2 and ½ tablespoons olive oil
- 1 small yellow onion, chopped
- 2 cups cauliflower florets chopped
- 2 tablespoons garlic, minced

Directions:
1. Lay out half of the chickpeas on a baking sheet lined with parchment pepper, add 1 tablespoon oil, season with salt and pepper, toss and bake at 400 degrees F for 30 minutes.
2. Transfer the chickpeas to a food processor, pulse well and put the mix into a bowl.
3. Heat up a pan with the ½ tablespoon oil over medium-high heat, add the garlic and the onion and sauté for 3 minutes.
4. Add the cauliflower, cook for 6 minutes more, transfer this to a blender, add the rest of the chickpeas, pulse, pour over the crispy chickpeas mix from the bowl, stir and shape medium fritters out of this mix.
5. Heat up a pan with the rest of the oil over medium-high heat, add the fritters, cook them for 3 minutes on each side and serve for breakfast.

Nutrition: 333 calories 12.6g fat 13.6g protein

56. Corn and Shrimp Salad

Preparation Time: 10 minutes
Cooking Time: 10 minutes
Servings: 4

Ingredients:
- 4 ears of sweet corn, husked
- 1 avocado, peeled, pitted and chopped
- ½ cup basil, chopped
- 1-pound shrimp, peeled and deveined
- 1 and ½ cups cherry tomatoes, halved

Directions:
1. Put the corn in a pot, boil water and cover, over medium heat for 6 minutes.
2. Drain, cool down, cut corn from the cob and put it in a bowl.
3. Thread the shrimp onto skewers and brush with some of the oil.
4. Place the skewers on the preheated grill, cook over medium heat for 2 minutes on each side, remove from skewers and add over the corn.
5. Place the rest of the ingredients to the bowl, toss, divide between plates and serve for breakfast.

Nutrition: 371 calories 22g fat 23g protein

57. Walnuts Yogurt Mix

Preparation Time: 10 minutes
Cooking Time: 0 minutes
Servings: 6

Ingredients:
- 2 and ½ cups Greek yogurt
- 1 and ½ cups walnuts, chopped
- 1 teaspoon vanilla extract
- ¾ cup honey
- 2 teaspoons cinnamon powder

Directions:
1. In a bowl, incorporate yogurt with the walnuts and the rest of the ingredients, toss, divide into smaller bowls and keep in the fridge for 10 minutes before serving for breakfast.

Nutrition: 388 calories 24.6g fat 10.2g protein

58. Tahini Pine Nuts Toast

Preparation Time: 5 minutes
Cooking Time: 0 minute
Servings: 2

Ingredients:
- 2 whole wheat bread slices, toasted
- 1 tablespoon tahini paste
- 2 teaspoons feta cheese, crumbled
- Juice of ½ lemon
- 2 teaspoons pine nuts

Directions:
1. Whisk tahini with the 1 tsp. of water and the lemon juice well and spread over the toasted bread slices.
2. Top each serving with the remaining ingredients and serve for breakfast.

Nutrition: 142 calories 7.6g fat 5.8g protein

59. Blueberries Quinoa

Preparation Time: 5 minutes
Cooking Time: 0 minutes
Servings: 4

Ingredients:
- 2 cups quinoa, almond milk
- ½ teaspoon cinnamon powder
- 1 tablespoon honey
- 1 cup blueberries
- ¼ cup walnuts, chopped

Directions:
1. In a bowl, scourge quinoa with the milk and the rest of the ingredients, toss, divide into smaller bowls and serve for breakfast.

Nutrition: 284 calories 14.3g fat 4.4g protein

61. Raspberries and Yogurt Smoothie

Preparation Time: 5 minutes
Cooking Time: 0 minutes
Servings: 2

Ingredients:
- 2 cups raspberries
- ½ cup Greek yogurt
- ½ cup almond milk
- ½ teaspoon vanilla extract

Directions:
1. In your blender, combine the raspberries with the milk, vanilla and the yogurt, pulse well, divide into 2 glasses and serve for breakfast.

Nutrition: 245 calories 9.5g fat 1.6g protein

62. Cottage Cheese and Berries Omelet

Preparation Time: 5 minutes
Cooking Time: 4 minutes
Servings: 1

Ingredients:
- 1 egg, whisked
- 1 teaspoon cinnamon powder
- 1 tablespoon almond milk
- 3 ounces cottage cheese
- 4 ounces blueberries

Directions:
1. Scourge egg with the rest of the ingredients except the oil and toss.
2. Preheat pan with the oil over medium heat, add the eggs mix, spread, cook for 2 minutes on each side, transfer to a plate and serve.

Nutrition: 190 calories 8g fat 2g protein

63. Salmon Frittata

Preparation Time: 5 minutes
Cooking Time: 27 minutes
Servings: 4

Ingredients:
- 1-pound gold potatoes, roughly cubed
- 1 tablespoon olive oil
- 2 salmon fillets, skinless and boneless
- 8 eggs, whisked
- 1 teaspoon mint, chopped

Directions:
1. Put the potatoes in a boiling water at medium heat, then cook for 12 minutes, drain and transfer to a bowl.
2. Arrange the salmon on a baking sheet lined with parchment paper, grease with cooking spray, and broil over medium-high heat for 5 minutes on each side, cool down, flake and put in a separate bowl.
3. Warm up a pan with the oil over medium heat, add the potatoes, salmon, and the rest of the ingredients except the eggs and toss.
4. Add the eggs on top, put the lid on and cook over medium heat for 10 minutes.
5. Divide the salmon between plates and serve.

Nutrition: 289 calories 11g fat 4g protein

64. Avocado and Olive Paste on Toasted Rye Bread

Preparation Time: 5 minutes
Cooking Time: 0 minute
Serving: 4

Ingredients:
- 1 avocado, halved, peeled and finely chopped
- 1 tbsp. green onions, finely chopped
- 2 tbsp. green olive paste
- 4 lettuce leaves
- 1 tbsp. lemon juice

Directions:
1. Crush avocados with a fork or potato masher until almost smooth. Add the onions, green olive paste and lemon juice. Season with salt and pepper to taste. Stir to combine.
2. Toast 4 slices of rye bread until golden. Spoon 1/4 of the avocado mixture onto each slice of bread, top with a lettuce leaf and serve.

Nutrition: 291 calories 13g fat 3g protein

66. Avocado and Chickpea Sandwiches

Preparation Time: 4 minutes
Cooking Time: 0 minute
Serving: 4

Ingredients:
- 1/2 cup canned chickpeas
- 1 small avocado
- 2 green onions, finely chopped
- 1 egg, hard boiled
- 1/2 tomato, cucumber

Directions:
1. Mash the avocado and chickpeas with a fork or potato masher until smooth. Add in green onions and salt and combine well. Spread this mixture on the four slices of bread. Top each slice with tomato, cucumber and egg, and serve.

Nutrition: 309 calories 9g fat 2g protein

67. Raisin Quinoa Breakfast

Preparation Time: 15 minutes
Cooking Time: 0 minute
Serving: 4

Ingredients:
- 1 cup quinoa
- 2 cups milk
- 2 tbsp. walnuts, crushed
- 2 tbsp. raisins, cranberries
- 1 tbsp. chia seeds

Directions:
1. Rinse quinoa with cold water and drain. Place milk and quinoa into a saucepan and bring to a boil. Add ½ tsp. of vanilla. Reduce heat to low and simmer for about 15 minutes stirring from time to time.
2. Set aside to cool then serve in a bowl, topped with honey, chia seeds, raisins, cranberries and crushed walnuts.

Nutrition: 299 calories 7g fat 1g protein

68. Banana Cinnamon Fritters

Preparation Time: 15 minutes
Cooking Time: 6 minutes
Serving: 4

Ingredients:
- 1 cup self-rising flour
- 1 egg, beaten
- 3/4 cup sparkling water
- 2 tsp ground cinnamon
- 2-3 bananas, cut diagonally into 4 pieces each

Directions:
1. Sift flour and cinnamon into a bowl and make a well in the center. Add egg and enough sparkling water to mix to a smooth batter.
2. Heat sunflower oil in a saucepan, enough to cover the base by 1-2 inch, so when a little batter dropped into the oil sizzles and rises to the surface. Dip banana pieces into the batter, then fry for 2-3 minutes or until golden. Pull out with a slotted spoon and drain on paper towels. Sprinkle with sugar and serve hot.

Nutrition: 209 calories 10g fat 2g protein

69. Veggie Casserole

Preparation Time: 25 minutes
Cooking Time: 45 minutes
Serving: 4

Ingredients:
- 1 lb. okra, trimmed
- 3 tomatoes, cut into wedges
- 3 garlic cloves, chopped
- 1 cup fresh parsley leaves, finely cut

Directions:
1. In a deep ovenproof baking dish, combine okra, sliced tomatoes, olive oil and garlic. Add in salt and black pepper to taste, and toss to combine. Bake in a prepared oven at 350 F for 45 minutes. Garnish with parsley and serve.

Nutrition: 302 calories 13g fat 6g protein

71. Ground Beef and Brussels Sprouts

Preparation Time: 20 minutes
Cooking Time: 36 minutes
Serving: 4

Ingredients:
- 6 oz. ground beef
- 2 garlic cloves, crushed
- ½ cup grated sweet potato
- 1 cup grated Brussels sprouts
- 1 egg, boiled

Directions:
1. In a medium saucepan, cook olive oil over medium heat. Gently sauté the ½ onion and garlic until the onion is soft and translucent. Add in the beef and the sweet potato and cook until the meat is fully cooked.
2. Stir in the Brussels sprouts and cook for about 5 minutes more. Season well and serve topped with a boiled egg.

Nutrition: 314 calories 15g fat 6g protein

72. Italian Mini Meatballs

Preparation Time: 13 minutes
Cooking Time: 20 minutes
Serving: 6

Ingredients:
- 1 lb. ground beef
- 1 onion, grated
- 1 egg, lightly whisked
- 1 tsp garlic powder
- 1 tsp dried basil, oregano, parsley

Directions:
1. Combine ground beef, onion, egg, parsley, garlic powder, basil and oregano. Mix very well with hands. Roll tablespoonfuls of the meat mixture into balls.
2. Place meatballs on a lined baking tray. Bake 20 minutes or until brown. Transfer to a serving plate and serve.

Nutrition: 275 calories 9g fat 1g protein

73. Mushroom and Olives Steaks

Preparation Time: 20 minutes
Cooking Time: 9 minutes
Serving: 6

Ingredients:
- 1 lb. boneless beef sirloin steak
- 1 large onion, sliced
- 5-6 white mushrooms
- 1/2 cup green olives, coarsely chopped
- 1 cup parsley leaves, finely cut

Directions:
1. Cook olive oil in a heavy bottomed pan at medium-high heat. Cook the steaks until well browned on each side then keep aside.
2. Gently sauté the onion in the same pan, for 3 minutes. Cook the mushrooms and olives until the mushrooms are done.
3. Return the steaks to the skillet, cover, and cook for 5-6 minutes. Stir in parsley and serve.

Nutrition: 281 calories 14g fat 3g protein

74. Salmon Kebabs

Preparation Time: 30 minutes
Cooking Time: 6 minutes
Serving: 5

Ingredients:
- 2 shallots, ends trimmed, halved
- 2 zucchinis, cut in 2-inch cubes
- 1 cup cherry tomatoes
- 6 skinless salmon fillets, cut into 1-inch pieces
- 3 limes, cut into thin wedges

Directions:
1. Preheat barbecue or char grill on medium-high. Thread fish cubes onto skewers, then zucchinis, shallots and tomatoes. Repeat to make 12 kebabs. Bake the kebabs for about 3 minutes each side for medium cooked.
2. Situate to a plate, wrap with foil and set aside for 5 minutes to rest.

Nutrition: 268 calories 9g fat 3g protein

76. Mediterranean Baked Salmon

Preparation Time: 35 minutes
Cooking Time: 11 minutes
Serving: 5

Ingredients:
- 2 (6 oz.) boneless salmon fillets
- 1 onion, tomato
- 1 tbsp. capers
- 1 tsp dry oregano
- 3 tbsp. Parmesan cheese

Direction:
1. Set oven to 350 F. Place the salmon fillets in a baking dish, sprinkle with oregano, top with onion and tomato slices, drizzle with olive oil, and sprinkle with capers and Parmesan cheese.
2. Wrap the dish with foil and bake for 30 minutes.

Nutrition: 291 calories 14g fat 2g protein

77. Feta Cheese Baked in Foil

Preparation Time: 15 minutes
Cooking Time: 16 minutes
Serving: 5

Ingredients:
- 14 oz. feta cheese, cut in slices
- 4 oz. butter
- 1 tbsp. paprika
- 1 tsp dried oregano

Directions:
1. Cut the cheese into four medium-thick slices and place on sheets of butter lined aluminum foil.
2. Place a little bit of butter on top each feta cheese piece, sprinkle with paprika and dried oregano and wrap. Place on a tray and bake in a preheated to 350 F oven for 15 minutes.

Nutrition: 279 calories 9g fat 2g protein

78. Avocado, Roasted Mushroom and Feta Spaghetti

Preparation Time: 20 minutes
Cooking Time: 17 minutes
Serving: 5

Ingredients:
- 12 oz. spaghetti
- 2 avocados, peeled and diced
- 10-15 white mushrooms, halved
- 1 cup feta, crumbled
- 2 tbsp. green olive paste

Direction
1. Wrap baking tray with baking paper and place mushrooms on it. Spray with olive oil and season with salt and black pepper to taste. Roast in a prepared to 375 F oven for 15 minutes.
2. In a big pot of boiling salted water, cook spaghetti following package's instructions. Drain and set aside.
3. In a blender, combine lemon juice, 2 garlic cloves, olive paste and avocados and blend until smooth.
4. Combine pasta, mushrooms and avocado sauce. Sprinkle with feta cheese and serve immediately.

Nutrition: 278 calories 10g fat 4g protein

79. Tomato, Arugula and Feta Spaghetti

Preparation Time: 20 minutes
Cooking Time: 3 minutes
Serving: 6

Ingredients:
- 12 oz. spaghetti
- 2 cups grape tomatoes, halved
- 1 cup fresh basil leaves, roughly torn
- 1 cup baby arugula leaves
- 1 cup feta, crumbled

Direction:
1. In a huge saucepan with salted boiling water, cook spaghetti according to package directions. Drain and keep aside.
2. Return saucepan to medium heat. Add olive oil, 2 garlic cloves and tomatoes. Season with pepper and cook, tossing, for 1-2 minutes or until tomatoes are hot. Add spaghetti, basil and

feta. Toss lightly for 1 minute. Sprinkle with arugula and serve.

Nutrition: 278 calories 15g fat 3g protein

Zucchini Fritters

Preparation Time: 20 minutes
Cooking Time: 26 minutes
Serving: 6

Ingredients:
- 5 zucchinis, grated
- 3 eggs
- 2 garlic cloves, crushed
- 5 spring onions, finely chopped
- 1 cup feta cheese, crumbled

Directions:
1. Grate zucchinis and situate them in a colander. Sprinkle with salt and leave aside to drain. After 20 minutes, squeeze and place in a bowl. Add in all other ingredients except for 1 cup of flour and sunflower oil. Combine everything very well. Add in flour and stir to combine again.
2. Cook sunflower oil in a frying pan. Drop a few scoops of the zucchini batter and fry them on medium heat for 3-5 minutes, until golden brown. Serve with yogurt.

Nutrition: 293 calories 13g fat 6g protein

80. Cheesy Cauliflower Florets

Preparation Time: 25 minutes
Cooking Time: 16 minutes
Serving: 6

Ingredients:
- 1 small cauliflower, cut into florets
- 1 tbsp. garlic powder
- 1 tsp paprika
- 4 tbsp. extra virgin olive oil
- 1/2 cup grated Parmesan cheese

Directions:
1. Combine olive oil, paprika, salt, pepper and garlic powder. Throw in the cauliflower florets and position in a baking dish in single layer.
2. Bake in a preheated to 350 F oven for 20 minutes. Pull out from the oven, stir, and topped with Parmesan cheese. Bake for 5 minutes more.

Nutrition: 297 calories 13g fat 6g protein

MAIN DISH RECIPES

81. Steak with Olives and Mushrooms

Preparation Time: 20 minutes
Cooking Time: 9 minutes
Serving: 6

Ingredients:
- lb. boneless beef sirloin steak
- 1 large onion, sliced
- 5-6 white button mushrooms
- 1/2 cup green olives, coarsely chopped
- 4 tbsp. extra virgin olive oil

Directions:
1. Heat olive oil in a heavy bottomed skillet over medium-high heat. Brown the steaks on both sides then put aside.
2. Gently sauté the onion in the same skillet, for 2-3 minutes, stirring rarely. Sauté in the mushrooms and olives.
3. Return the steaks to the skillet, cover, cook for 5-6 minutes and serve.

Nutrition: 299 calories 56g fat 16g protein

82. Spicy Mustard Chicken

Preparation Time: 32 minutes
Cooking Time: 36 minutes
Serving: 4

Ingredients:
- 4 chicken breasts
- 2 garlic cloves, crushed
- 1/3 cup chicken broth
- 3 tbsp. Dijon mustard
- tsp chili powder

Directions:
1. In a small bowl, mix the mustard, chicken broth, garlic and chili. Marinate the chicken for 30 minutes.
2. Bake in a preheated to 375 F oven for 35 minutes.

Nutrition: 302 calories 18g fat 49g protein

83. Walnut and Oregano Crusted Chicken

Preparation Time: 36 minutes
Cooking Time: 13 minutes
Serving: 4

Ingredients:
- 4 skinless, boneless chicken breasts
- 10-12 fresh oregano leaves
- 1/2 cup walnuts, chopped
- 2 garlic cloves, chopped
- 2 eggs, beaten

Directions:
1. Blend the garlic, oregano and walnuts in a food processor until a rough crumb is formed. Place this mixture on a plate.
2. Whisk eggs in a deep bowl. Soak each chicken breast in the beaten egg then roll it in the walnut mixture. Place coated chicken on a baking tray and bake at 375 F for 13 minutes each side.

Nutrition: 304 calories 54g fat 14g protein

84. Chicken and Onion Casserole

Preparation Time: 16 minutes
Cooking Time: 47 minutes
Serving: 4

Ingredients:
- 4 chicken breasts
- 4-5 large onions, sliced
- 2 leeks, cut
- 4 tbsp. extra virgin olive oil
- 1 tsp thyme

Directions:
1. Cook olive oil in a large, deep frying pan over medium-high heat. Brown chicken, turning, for 2-3 minutes each side or until golden. Set aside in a casserole dish.
2. Cut the onions and leeks and add them on and around the chicken, Add in olives, thyme, salt and black pepper to taste. Cover it using aluminum foil and bake at 375 F for 35 minutes, or until the chicken is cooked through. Uncover and return to the oven for 5 minutes or until chicken is crispy.

Nutrition: 309 calories 59g fat 18g protein

85. Chicken and Mushrooms

Preparation Time: 20 minutes
Cooking Time: 7 minutes
Serving: 4

Ingredients:
- 4 chicken breasts, diced
- 2 lbs. mushrooms, chopped
- onion, chopped
- 4 tbsp. extra virgin olive oil
- salt and black, pepper to taste

Directions:
1. Heat olive oil in a deep-frying pan over medium-high heat. Brown chicken, stirring, for 2 minutes each side, or until golden. Add the chopped onion, mushrooms, salt and black pepper, and stir to combine. Reduce heat, cover and simmer for 30 minutes. Uncover and simmer for 5 more minutes.

Nutrition: 290 calories 49g fat 9g protein

86. Blue Cheese and Mushroom Chicken

Preparation Time: 25 minutes
Cooking Time: 18 minutes
Serving: 4

Ingredients:
- 4 chicken breast halves
- cup crumbled blue cheese
- 1 cup sour cream
- salt and black pepper, to taste
- 1/2 cup parsley, finely cut

Direction:
1. Prep the oven to 350 degrees F. Grease a casserole with nonstick spray. Place all ingredients into it, turn chicken to coat.
2. Bake for 20 minutes or until chicken juices run clear. Sprinkle with parsley and serve.

Nutrition: 287 calories 46g fat 10g protein

87. Herb-Roasted Lamb Leg

Preparation Time: 14 minutes
Cooking Time: 2 hours
Serving: 4

Ingredients:
- (6-lb) boneless leg of lamb, trimmed
- cups fresh spinach leaves
- 1/3 cup water
- tbsp. Italian seasoning
- tbsp. extra virgin olive oil

Directions:
1. Combine spinach, Italian seasoning and olive oil in a food processor. Process until finely minced.
2. Thoroughly coat the top and sides of the lamb with this mixture.
3. Place in the bottom of a large roasting pan. Add water and cook, covered, at 300 F for approximately two hours or until cooked through.
4. Uncover and cook for 10 minutes more.

Nutrition: 309 calories 41g fat 12g protein

88. Spring Lamb Stew

Preparation Time: 34 minutes
Cooking Time: 13 minutes
Serving: 4

Ingredients:
- lb. lamb, cubed
- 1 lb. white mushrooms, chopped
- 4 cups fresh spring onions, chopped
- tbsp. extra virgin olive oil
- 1 tbsp. Italian seasoning

Directions:
1. Heat olive oil in a deep casserole. Gently brown lamb pieces for 2-3 minutes. Add in the mushrooms and cook for a minute more, stirring.
2. Stir in Italian seasoning, cover, and cook for an hour or until tender. Add in spring onions and simmer for 10 minutes more.
3. Uncover and cook until almost all the liquid evaporates.

Nutrition: 309 calories 41g fat 10g protein

89. Balsamic Roasted Carrots and Baby Onions

Preparation Time: 50 minutes
Cooking Time: 26 minutes
Serving: 4

Ingredients:
- 2 bunches baby carrots, scrubbed, ends trimmed
- 10 small onions, peeled, halved
- 4 tbsp. 100% pure maple syrup (unprocessed)
- tsp thyme
- tbsp. extra virgin olive oil

Directions:
1. Preheat oven to 350F. Line a baking tray with baking paper.
2. Place the carrots, onion, thyme and oil in a large bowl and toss until well coated. Spread carrots and onion, in a single layer, on the baking tray. Roast for 25 minutes or until tender.
3. Sprinkle over the maple syrup and vinegar and toss to coat. Roast for 25-30 minutes more or until vegetables are tender and caramelized. Season well and serve.

Nutrition: 401 calories 49g fat 20g protein

90. Baked Cauliflower

Preparation Time: 13 minutes
Cooking Time: 26 minutes
Serving: 4

Ingredients:
- small cauliflower, cut into florets
- 1 tbsp. garlic powder
- 1 tsp paprika
- 4 tbsp. extra virgin olive oil
- grated Parmesan cheese, to taste

Directions:
1. Combine olive oil, paprika and garlic powder together. Mix in the cauliflower florets and situate in a baking dish in one layer.
2. Bake in a preheated to 350 F oven for 20 minutes. Take away from the oven, and drizzle with Parmesan cheese. Cook for 5 minutes more.

Nutrition: 316 calories 53g fat 17g protein

91. Baked Bean and Rice Casserole

Preparation Time: 8 minutes
Cooking Time: 22 minutes
Serving: 4

Ingredients:
- can red beans, rinsed
- 1 cup water
- 2/3 cup rice
- onions, chopped
- tsp dried mint

Directions:
1. Cook olive oil in an ovenproof casserole dish and gently sauté the chopped onions for 1-2 minutes. Stir in the rice and cook, stirring constantly, for another minute.
2. Rinse the beans and add them to the casserole. Stir in a cup of water and the mint and bake in a preheated to 350 F oven for 20 minutes.

Nutrition: 405 calories 49g fat 12g protein

92. Okra and Tomato Casserole

Preparation Time: 25 minutes
Cooking Time: 26 minutes
Serving: 4

Ingredients:
- lb. okra, trimmed
- tomatoes, cut into wedges
- garlic cloves, chopped
- 1 cup fresh parsley leaves, finely cut
- tbsp. extra virgin olive oil

Directions:
1. In a deep ovenproof baking dish, combine okra, sliced tomatoes, olive oil and garlic.
2. Toss to combine and bake in a preheated to 350 degrees F oven for 45 minutes. Drizzle with parsley and serve.

Nutrition: 304 calories 48g fat 13g protein

94. Spicy Baked Feta with Tomatoes

Preparation Time: 15 minutes
Cooking Time: 22 minutes
Serving: 4

Ingredients:
- lb. feta cheese, cut in slices
- ripe tomatoes, sliced
- 1 onion, sliced
- tbsp. extra virgin olive oil
- 1/2 tbsp. hot paprika

Directions:
1. Preheat the oven to 430F
2. In an ovenproof baking dish, arrange the slices of onions and tomatoes overlapping slightly but not too much. Sprinkle with olive oil.
3. Bake for 5 minutes then place the feta slices on top of the vegetables. Sprinkle with hot paprika. Bake for 15 more minutes and serve.

Nutrition: 303 calories 46g fat 12g protein

95. Baked Lemon-Butter Fish

Preparation Time: 10 minutes
Cooking Time: 17 minutes
Serving: 4

Ingredients:
- 4 tablespoons butter, plus more for coating
- 2 (5-ounce) tilapia fillets
- 2 garlic cloves, minced
- lemon, zested and juiced
- tablespoons capers, rinsed and chopped

Direction
1. Preheat the oven to 400°F. Coat an 8-inch baking dish with butter.
2. Pat dry the tilapia with paper towels, and season on both sides with pink Himalayan salt and pepper. Place in the greased baking dish.
3. In a medium skillet at medium heat, heat up butter. Add the garlic and cook for 3 to 5 minutes, until slightly browned but not burned.
4. Remove the garlic butter from the heat, and mix in the lemon zest and 2 tablespoons of lemon juice.
5. Pour the lemon-butter sauce over the fish, and sprinkle the capers around the baking pan.
6. Bake for 13 minutes and serve.

Nutrition: 299 Calories 26g Fat 1g Fiber

96. Fish Taco Bowl

Preparation Time: 10 minutes
Cooking Time: 15 minutes
Serving: 2

Ingredients:
- 2 (5-ounce) tilapia fillets
- 4 teaspoons Tajin seasoning salt, divided
- cups pre-sliced coleslaw cabbage mix
- 1 tablespoon Spicy Red Pepper Miso Mayo, plus more for serving
- 1 avocado, mashed

Direction
1. Preheat the oven to 425°F. Prep baking sheet with silicone baking mat.
2. Rub the tilapia with the olive oil, and then coat it with 2 teaspoons of Tajin seasoning salt. Place the fish in the prepared pan.
3. Bake for 15 minutes, or until the fish is opaque when you pierce it with a fork. Put the fish on a cooling rack and let it sit for 4 minutes.
4. Meanwhile, in a medium bowl, gently mix to combine the coleslaw and the mayo sauce. You don't want the cabbage super wet, just enough to dress it. Add the mashed avocado and the remaining 2 teaspoons of Tajin seasoning salt to the coleslaw, and season with pink Himalayan salt and pepper. Divide the salad between two bowls.
5. Shred the fish into small pieces, and add it to the bowls.
6. Top the fish with a drizzle of mayo sauce and serve.

Nutrition: 315 Calories 24g Fat 7g Fiber

97. Scallops with Creamy Bacon Sauce

Preparation Time: 5 minutes
Cooking Time: 20 minutes
Serving: 2

Ingredients:
- 4 bacon slices
- cup heavy (whipping) cream
- ¼ cup grated Parmesan cheese
- 1 tablespoon ghee
- 8 large sea scallops, rinsed and patted dry

Direction
1. In a medium skillet at medium-high heat, fry bacon on both sides for 8 minutes. Transfer the bacon to a paper towel–lined plate.
2. Lower the heat to medium. Add the cream, butter, and Parmesan cheese to the bacon grease, and season with a pinch of pink Himalayan salt and pepper. Decrease the heat to low and cook, stir constantly, for 10 minutes.
3. In a separate large skillet over medium-high heat, heat the ghee until sizzling.
4. Season the scallops with pink Himalayan salt and pepper, and add them to the skillet. Cook for just 1 minute per side. Do not crowd the scallops; if your pan isn't large enough, cook them in two batches. You want the scallops golden on each side.
5. Transfer the scallops to a paper towel–lined plate.
6. Divide the cream sauce between two plates, crumble the bacon on top of the cream sauce, and top with 4 scallops each. Serve immediately.

Nutrition: 782 Calories 73g Fat 24g Protein

98. Shrimp and Avocado Lettuce Cups

Preparation Time: 10 minutes
Cooking Time: 5 minutes
Serving: 2

Ingredients:
- tablespoon ghee
- ½ pound shrimp
- ½ avocado, sliced
- 4 butter lettuce leaves
- 1 tablespoon Spicy Red Pepper Miso Mayo

Direction
1. Preheat medium skillet over medium-high heat, cook the ghee. Add the shrimp and cook. Season with pink Himalayan salt and pepper. Shrimp are cooked when they turn pink and opaque.
2. Season the tomatoes and avocado with pink Himalayan salt and pepper.
3. Divide the lettuce cups between two plates. Fill each cup with shrimp, ½ cup grape tomatoes, and avocado. Drizzle the mayo sauce on top and serve.

Nutrition: 326 Calories 11g Fat 3g Fiber

99. Garlic Butter Shrimp

Preparation Time: 10 minutes
Cooking Time: 15 minutes
Serving: 2

Ingredients:
- 3 tablespoons butter
- ½ pound shrimp
- lemon, halved
- garlic cloves, crushed
- ¼ teaspoon red pepper flakes (optional)

Direction
1. Preheat the oven to 425°F.
2. Place the butter in an 8-inch baking dish, and pop it into the oven while it is preheating, just until the butter melts.
3. Sprinkle the shrimp with pink Himalayan salt and pepper.
4. Slice one half of the lemon in thin slices, and cut the other half into 2 wedges.
5. In the baking dish, add the shrimp and garlic to the butter. The shrimp should be in a single layer. Add the lemon slices. Sprinkle the top of the fish with the red pepper flakes (if using).
6. Bake the shrimp for 15 minutes, stirring halfway through.
7. Remove the shrimp from the oven, and squeeze juice from the 2 lemon wedges over the dish. Serve hot.

Nutrition: 329 Calories 20g Fat 32g Protein

100. Parmesan-Garlic Salmon with Asparagus

Preparation Time: 10 minutes
Cooking Time: 15 minutes
Serving: 2

Ingredients:
- 2 (6-ounce) salmon fillets, skin on
- pound fresh asparagus, ends snapped off
- tablespoons butter
- garlic cloves, minced
- ¼ cup grated Parmesan cheese

Direction:
1. Preheat the oven to 400°F. Prepare baking sheet with silicone baking mat.
2. Pat dry the salmon using paper towel, and season both sides with pink Himalayan salt and pepper.
3. Situate the salmon in the middle of the prepared pan, and arrange the asparagus around the salmon.
4. In a small saucepan over medium heat, melt the butter. Add the minced garlic and stir until the garlic just begins to brown, about 3 minutes.
5. Drizzle the garlic-butter sauce over the salmon and asparagus, and top both with the Parmesan cheese.
6. Bake until the salmon is cooked and the asparagus is crisp-tender, about 12 minutes. You can switch the oven to broil at the end of cooking time for about 3 minutes to get a nice char on the asparagus.
7. Serve hot.

Nutrition: 434 Calories 26g Fat 42g Protein

101. Seared-Salmon Shirataki Rice Bowls

Preparation Time: 40 minutes
Cooking Time: 10 minutes
Serving: 2

Ingredients:
- 2 (6-ounce) salmon fillets, skin on
- 4 tablespoons soy sauce (or coconut aminos), divided
- 2 small Persian cucumbers or ½ large English cucumber
- 1 (8-ounce) pack Miracle Shirataki Rice
- 1 avocado, diced

Direction
1. Place the salmon in an 8-inch baking dish, and add 3 tablespoons of soy sauce. Cover and marinate in the refrigerator for 30 minutes.
2. Meanwhile, slice the cucumbers thin, put them in a small bowl, and add the remaining 1 tablespoon of soy sauce. Set aside to marinate.
3. Situate skillet over medium heat, melt the ghee. Add the salmon fillets skin-side down. Pour some of the soy sauce marinade over the salmon, and sear the fish for 3 to 4 minutes on each side.
4. Meanwhile, in a large saucepan, cook the shirataki rice per package instructions:
5. Rinse the shirataki rice in cold water in a colander.
6. In a saucepan filled with boiling water, cook the rice for 2 minutes.
7. Pour the rice into the colander. Dry out the pan.
8. Transfer the rice to the dry pan and dry roast over medium heat until dry and opaque.
9. Season the avocado with pink Himalayan salt and pepper.
10. Place the salmon fillets on a plate, and remove the skin. Cut the salmon into bite-size pieces.
11. Assemble the rice bowls: In two bowls, make a layer of the cooked Miracle Rice. Top each with the cucumbers, avocado, and salmon, and serve.

Nutrition: 328 Calories 18g Fat 36g Protein

102. Pork Rind Salmon Cakes

Preparation Time: 10 minutes
Cooking Time: 10 minutes
Serving: 2

Ingredients
- 6 ounces canned Alaska wild salmon, drained
- 2 tablespoons crushed pork rinds
- egg, lightly beaten
- 1 tablespoon ghee
- ½ tablespoon Dijon mustard

Direction:
1. In a medium bowl, incorporate salmon, pork rinds, egg, and 1½ tablespoons of mayonnaise, and season with pink Himalayan salt and pepper.
2. With the salmon mixture, form patties the size of hockey pucks or smaller. Keep patting the patties until they keep together.
3. Position the medium skillet over medium-high heat, melt the ghee. When the ghee sizzles, place

the salmon patties in the pan. Cook for 6 minutes both sides. Transfer the patties to a paper towel–lined plate.
4. In a small bowl, mix together the remaining 1½ tablespoons of mayonnaise and the mustard.
5. Serve the salmon cakes with the mayo-mustard dipping sauce.

Nutrition: 362 Calories 31g Fat 24g Protein

103. Creamy Dill Salmon

Preparation Time: 10 minutes
Cooking Time: 10 minutes
Serving: 2

Ingredients:
- 2 tablespoons ghee, melted
- 2 (6-ounce) salmon fillets, skin on
- ¼ cup mayonnaise
- tablespoon Dijon mustard
- tablespoons minced fresh dill

Direction:
1. Preheat the oven to 450°F. Grease 9-by-13-inch baking dish with the ghee.
2. Pat salmon dry with paper towels, season on both sides with pink Himalayan salt and pepper, and place in the prepared baking dish.
3. In a small bowl, mix to combine the mayonnaise, mustard, dill, and garlic powder.
4. Slather the mayonnaise sauce on top of both salmon fillets so that it fully covers the tops.
5. Bake depending on how you like your salmon— 7 minutes for medium-rare and 9 minutes for well-done—and serve.

Nutrition: 510 Calories 41g Fat 33g Protein

104. Chicken-Basil Alfredo with Shirataki Noodles

Preparation Time: 10 minutes
Cooking Time: 15 minutes
Serving: 2

Ingredients:
For noodles
- (7-ounce) package Miracle Noodle Fettuccini Shirataki Noodles

For sauce
- 4 ounces cooked shredded chicken (I usually use a store-bought rotisserie chicken)
- 1 cup Alfredo Sauce, or any brand you like
- ¼ cup grated Parmesan cheese
- tablespoons chopped fresh basil leaves

Direction:
For noodles
1. Follow the instructions on the package:
2. In a colander, rinse the noodles with cold water (shirataki noodles naturally have a smell, and rinsing with cold water will help remove this).
3. Boil water in a large saucepan over high heat. Boil noodles for 2 minutes. Drain.
4. Transfer the noodles to a dry skillet over medium-low heat to evaporate any moisture. Do not grease the skillet; it must be dry. Situate to a plate and set aside.

For sauce
5. Situate saucepan over medium heat, heat the olive oil. Add the cooked chicken. Season with pink Himalayan salt and pepper.
6. Pour the Alfredo sauce over the chicken, and cook until warm. Season with more pink Himalayan salt and pepper.
7. Add the dried noodles to the sauce mixture, and toss until combined.
8. Divide the pasta between two plates, top each with the Parmesan cheese and chopped basil, and serve.

Nutrition: 673 Calories 61g Fat 29g Protein

105. Chicken Quesadilla

Preparation Time: 5 minutes
Cooking Time: 5 minutes
Serving: 2

Ingredients:
- low-carbohydrate tortillas
- ½ cup shredded Mexican blend cheese
- ounces shredded chicken (I usually use a store-bought rotisserie chicken)
- 1 teaspoon Tajin seasoning salt
- 2 tablespoons sour cream

Direction
1. In a big skillet at medium-high heat, cook olive oil. Add a tortilla, then layer on top ¼ cup of cheese, the chicken, the Tajin seasoning, and the remaining ¼ cup of cheese. Top with the second tortilla.
2. Peek under the edge of the bottom tortilla to monitor how it is browning. Once the bottom tortilla gets golden and the cheese begins to melt, after about 2 minutes, flip the quesadilla over. The second side will cook faster, about 1 minute.

3. Once the second tortilla is crispy and golden, transfer the quesadilla to a cutting board and let sit for 2 minutes. Cut the quesadilla into 4 wedges using a pizza cutter or chef's knife.
4. Transfer half the quesadilla to each of two plates. Add 1 tablespoon of sour cream to each plate, and serve hot.

Nutrition: 414 Calories 28g Fat 17g Fiber

106. Garlic-Parmesan Chicken Wings

Preparation Time: 10 minutes
Cooking Time: 3 hours
Serving: 2

Ingredients:
- 8 tablespoons (1 stick) butter
- 2 garlic cloves, minced
- tablespoon dried Italian seasoning
- ¼ cup grated Parmesan cheese, plus ½ cup
- 1-pound chicken wings

Direction:
1. With the crock insert in place, preheat the slow cooker to high. Cover baking sheet with silicone baking mat.
2. Put the butter, garlic, Italian seasoning, and ¼ cup of Parmesan cheese in the slow cooker, and season with pink Himalayan salt and pepper. Heat up the butter, and stir the ingredients until well mixed.
3. Add the chicken wings and stir until coated with the butter mixture.
4. Cover the slow cooker and cook for 2 hours and 45 minutes.
5. Preheat the broiler.
6. Transfer the wings to the prepared baking sheet, sprinkle the remaining ½ cup of Parmesan cheese over the wings, and cook under the broiler until crispy, about 5 minutes.
7. Serve hot.

Nutrition: 738 Calories 66g Fat 39g Protein

107. Chicken Skewers with Peanut Sauce

Preparation Time: 70 minutes
Cooking Time: 15 minutes
Serving: 2

Ingredients:

- 1-pound boneless skinless chicken breast, cut into chunks
- 3 tablespoons soy sauce (or coconut aminos), divided
- ½ teaspoon Sriracha sauce, plus ¼ teaspoon
- 3 teaspoons toasted sesame oil, divided
- 2 tablespoons peanut butter

Direction:
1. In a large zip-top bag, mix chicken chunks with 2 tablespoons of soy sauce, ½ teaspoon of Sriracha sauce, and 2 teaspoons of sesame oil. Seal, and marinate for an hour or so in the refrigerator or up to overnight.
2. If you are using wooden 8-inch skewers, soak them in water for 30 minutes before using.
3. Preheat your grill pan or grill to low. Oil the grill pan with ghee.
4. Thread the chicken chunks onto the skewers.
5. Cook the skewers over low heat for 10 to 15 minutes, flipping halfway through.
6. Meanwhile, mix the peanut dipping sauce. Stir together the remaining 1 tablespoon of soy sauce, ¼ teaspoon of Sriracha sauce, 1 teaspoon of sesame oil, and the peanut butter. Season with pink Himalayan salt and pepper.
7. Serve the chicken skewers with a small dish of the peanut sauce.

Nutrition: 586 Calories 29g Fat 75g Protein

108. Braised Chicken Thighs with Kalamata Olives

Preparation Time: 10 minutes
Cooking Time: 40 minutes
Serving: 4

Ingredients:
- 4 chicken thighs, skin on
- 2 tablespoons ghee
- ½ cup chicken broth
- lemon, ½ sliced and ½ juiced
- ½ cup pitted Kalamata olives

Direction:
1. Preheat the oven to 375 degrees F.
2. Pat the chicken thighs dry using paper towels, and season with pink Himalayan salt and pepper.
3. In a medium oven-safe skillet or high-sided baking dish over medium-high heat, melt the ghee. When the ghee has melted and is hot, add the chicken thighs, skin-side down, and leave

Direction
1. Pat your lamb chop dry using a kitchen towel and arrange them on a shallow glass baking dish
2. Take a bowl and a whisk in Dijon mustard, balsamic vinegar, pepper and mix them well
3. Whisk in the oil very slowly into the marinade until the mixture is smooth
4. Stir in basil
5. Pour the marinade over the lamb chops and stir to coat both sides well
6. Cover the chops and allow them to marinate for 1-4 hours (chilled)
7. Get the chops out and leave them for 30 minutes to allow the temperature to reach a normal level
8. Pre-heat your grill to medium heat and add oil to the grate
9. Grill the lamb chops for 5-10 minutes per side until both sides are browned
10. Once the center reads 145 degrees Fahrenheit the chops are ready, serve and enjoy!

Nutrition: 521 Calories 45g Fat 3.5g Carbohydrates

117. Amazingly Baked Chicken Breast

Preparation Time: 10 minutes
Cooking Time: 40 minutes
Serving: 2

Ingredients
- 2 pieces of 8 ounces skinless and boneless chicken breast
- Salt and pepper as needed
- ¼ cup of olive oil and lemon juice (equal amount)
- ½ a teaspoon of dried oregano
- ¼ teaspoon of dried thyme

Direction
1. Season breast by rubbing salt and pepper on all sides
2. Transfer the chicken to a bowl
3. Take another bowl and add olive oil, oregano, lemon juice, thyme and mix well
4. Pour the prepared marinade over the chicken breast and allow it to marinate for 10 minutes
5. Pre-heat your oven to 400 degrees Fahrenheit
6. Set the oven rack about 6 inches above the heat source
7. Transfer the chicken breast to a baking sheet and pour extra marinade on top
8. Bake for 40 minutes
9. Remove it and place it on the top rack
10. Broil for 5 minutes more

Nutrition: 501 Calories 32g Fat 3.5g Carbohydrates

118. Homely Tuscan Tuna Salad

Preparation Time: 8 minutes
Cooking Time: 0 minute
Serving: 4

Ingredients
- 15 ounces small white beans
- 6 ounces drained chunks of light tuna
- 10 cherry tomatoes, quartered
- 4 scallions, trimmed and sliced
- 2 tablespoons lemon juice

Direction
1. Stir all the ingredients to a bowl
2. Season with salt and pepper accordingly, enjoy!

Nutrition: 322 Calories 8g Fat 32g Carbohydrates

119. Cool Garbanzo and Spinach Beans

Preparation Time: 9 minutes
Cooking Time: 0 minute
Serving: 4

Ingredients
- tablespoon olive oil
- ½ onion, diced
- 10 ounces spinach, chopped
- 12 ounces garbanzo beans
- ½ teaspoon cumin

Direction
1. Take a skillet and add olive oil, let it warm over medium-low heat
2. Add onions, garbanzo and cook for 5 minutes
3. Stir in spinach, cumin, garbanzo beans and season with salt
4. Use a spoon to smash gently
5. Cook thoroughly until heated, enjoy!

Nutrition: 90 Calories 4g Fat 11g Carbohydrates

121. Clean Eating Medi Stuffed Chicken Breasts

Preparation Time: 7 minutes
Cooking Time: 28 minutes
Serving: 4

Ingredients
- 8 ounces chicken breast
- large red bell pepper
- tablespoons Kalamata olives, chopped
- ¼ cup feta cheese, crumbled
- 1 tablespoon fresh basil

Direction
1. Prepare your broiler to high heat
2. Slice bell pepper in half lengthwise and discard membrane and seeds.
3. Take a baking sheet and place pepper halves, skin side up, flatten with hand
4. Place pepper into the oven and broil for 15 minutes until blackened
5. Once done, place peppers in a Ziplock bag and let them sit for 15 minutes
6. Peel peppers and chop them
7. Once done, place a pan on grill over medium-high heat
8. Add cheese, olives, basil and bell pepper
9. Slice horizontal slits through the thickest part of the chicken and make a sort of pocket
10. Once done, place pepper mixture into the slits and close the pockets, secure using a wooden toothpick
11. Season with salt and pepper
12. Grill both sides for 7 minutes each until thoroughly cooked
13. Once done, let it stand for 10 minutes, enjoy!

Nutrition: 210 Calories 6g Fat 32g Protein

122. Lemony Garlic Shrimp

Preparation Time: 7 minutes
Cooking Time: 16 minutes
Serving: 4

Ingredients
- 1 ¼ pounds shrimp, boiled or steamed
- tablespoons garlic, minced
- ¼ cup lemon juice
- tablespoons olive oil
- ¼ cup parsley

Direction
1. Preheat skillet over medium heat, add garlic and oil and stir cook for 1 minute
2. Add parsley, lemon juice and season with salt and pepper accordingly
3. Add shrimp in a large bowl and transfer the mixture from the skillet over the shrimp
4. Chill and serve

Nutrition: 130 Calories 3g Fat 2g Carbohydrates

123. Completely Herbed Up Feisty Baby Potatoes

Preparation Time: 10 minutes
Cooking Time: 35 minutes
Serving: 4

Ingredients
- 2 pounds new yellow potatoes, scrubbed and cut into wedges
- 2 tablespoons extra virgin olive oil
- 2 teaspoons fresh rosemary, chopped
- teaspoon garlic powder
- ½ teaspoon freshly ground black pepper and salt

Direction
1. Pre-heat your oven to 400 degrees Fahrenheit
2. Spread the foil onto the baking sheet and set it aside
3. Take a large bowl and add potatoes, olive oil, garlic, rosemary, sea salt and pepper
4. Spread potatoes in single layer on baking sheet and bake for 35 minutes
5. Serve and enjoy!

Nutrition: 225 Calories 7g Fat: 37g Carbohydrates

124. Mediterranean Kale Dish

Preparation Time: 15 minutes
Cooking Time: 10 minutes
Serving: 6

Ingredients
- 12 cups kale, chopped
- 2 tablespoons lemon juice
- tablespoon olive oil
- 1 teaspoon soy sauce
- Salt and pepper as needed

Direction
1. Add a steamer insert to your Saucepan
2. Fill in the saucepan with water up to the bottom of the steamer
3. Cover and bring water to boil (medium-high heat)
4. Add kale to the insert and steam for 7-8 minutes
5. Take a large bowl and add lemon juice, olive oil, salt, soy sauce, and pepper
6. Mix well and add the steamed kale to the bowl
7. Toss and serve

Nutrition: 350 Calories 17g Fat 41g Carbohydrates

125. Yogurt Marinated Tenderloin

Preparation Time: 8 minutes
Cooking Time: 30 minutes
Serving: 6

Ingredients:
- 2 Pork Tenderloins, 10-12 Ounces Each
- ¼ Cup Greek Yogurt, 2%
- 1 Tablespoon Rosemary, Fresh & Chopped
- Tzatziki Sauce
- 2 Tablespoons Mint, Fresh & Chopped

Directions:
1. Start by heating the oven to 500.
2. Take huge baking sheet and line it with foil with a wire rack on top. Spray the rack down with oil.
3. Put both pieces of pork on the rack, and season with salt and pepper.
4. Get out a bowl and mix your yogurt and rosemary together and coat on all sides.
5. Roast for ten minutes.
6. Remove it from the oven, and then turn it over.
7. Roast for ten to twelve more minutes.
8. Remove the pork from the rack and cut. Allow it to rest for five minutes before slicing.
9. Serve with tzatziki and mint leaves.

Nutrition: 183 Calories 22g Protein 10g Fat

126. Buttery Herb Lamb Chops

Preparation Time: 11 minutes
Cooking Time: 20 minutes
Serving: 4

Ingredients:
- 8 Lamb Chops
- 1 Tablespoon Olive Oil
- 1 Tablespoon Butter
- 4 Ounces Herb Butter
- 1 Lemon, Cut into Wedges

Directions:
1. Season your lamb chops well, and then get out a pan.
2. Heat up butter in a pan over medium-high heat and then fry your chops for four minutes per side.
3. Arrange on a serving plate with herb butter on each one. Serve with a lemon wedge.

Nutrition: 729 Calories 43g Protein 62g Fat

SIDE RECIPES

127. Lemon Fruit and Nut Bars

Preparation Time: 15 minutes
Cooking Time: 0 minute
Servings: 10

Ingredients
- ½ Cup Raw Almonds
- ¾ Cup Raw Cashews
- 1 Cup Deglet Noor Dates
- 1 Lemon – Juice and Zest

Direction
1. Ground cashews and almonds in a nourishment processor until they are finely cut. Add dates, lemon juice, and lemon pieces. Beat until all ingredients are mixed.
2. Pour blend between two sheets of cling wrap. Utilize your hands to press and frame the blend into a minimized rectangular shape.
3. Fold the saran wrap over it and refrigerate for 2 hours. This will enable it to solidify and make it simpler to cut into bars.
4. Remove from the cooler and cut into 10 bars. Envelop the bars with cling wrap and store them in the ice chest.

Nutrition: 132 Calories 6.5g Fat 3.2g Protein

128. Cauliflower Fried Rice with Bacon

Preparation Time: 5 minutes
Cooking Time: 10 minutes
Servings: 4

Ingredients:
- 4 slices bacon
- 1 small onion
- 1 head cauliflower
- 1 cup frozen mixed vegetables
- 1 tsp Bragg's Liquid Amino

Direction
1. In a wok or enormous sauté container over medium flame, cook bacon.
2. Add the onions and pan-fried food until translucent.
3. Set heat to high. Add the shredded cauliflower and pan-fried food for 1 moment. Add water and mixed vegetables, mix well, spread the dish and let the cauliflower blend steam for an additional 3 minutes or until tender.
4. Add Bragg's Liquid Amino. Taste and add salt for extra flavoring as wanted.

Nutrition: 315 Calories 25g Fat 19g Protein

129. Halloumi Cheese with Butter-Fried Eggplant

Preparation Time: 5 minutes
Cooking Time: 10 minutes
Serving: 2

Ingredients
- 1 eggplant
- 3 oz. butter
- 10 oz. halloumi cheese
- 10 black olives
- salt and pepper

Direction:
1. Cut the eggplant down the middle, longwise, and cut into pieces which are a big portion and an inch thick.
2. Heat up a healthful dab of butter in an enormous pan.
3. Add the cheese on one side of the dish and eggplant on the other. Season eggplant with salt and pepper
4. Fry over medium-high heat for 5-7mins. Flip the cheese after three minutes, with the aim that it's darker on the 2 sides.
5. Mix the eggplant now.
6. Present with olives.

Nutrition: 829 Calories 72g Fat 32g Protein

130. White Lasagna Stuffed Peppers

Preparation Time: 5 minutes
Cooking Time: 1 hour
Serving: 4

Ingredients
- 2 large sweet peppers
- 1 tsp garlic salt
- 12 oz. ground turkey
- 3/4 cup ricotta cheese
- 1 cup mozzarella

Direction
1. Preheat stove to 400.
2. Put the cut peppers in a heating dish. Sprinkle with 1/4 tsp garlic salt. Gap the ground turkey between the peppers. Sprinkle with another 1/4 tsp garlic salt. Cook for 30 minutes.
3. Partition the ricotta cheese between the peppers. Sprinkle with 1/2 tsp garlic salt. Sprinkle the mozzarella on top. Put the cherry tomatoes in the middle of the peppers, if utilizing.
4. Cook for an extra 30 minutes until the meat is cooked, and the cheese is golden.

Nutrition: 281 Calories 14g Fat 32g Protein

131. Boiled Eggs with Butter and Thyme

Preparation Time: 10 minutes
Cooking Time: 6 minutes
Servings: 1

Ingredients
- 3 large eggs
- 1 tbsp. good quality unsalted butter
- Freshly ground black pepper
- Salt
- 1/4 tsp thyme leaves

Direction
1. Fill a medium pan most of the way with water and heat until boiling.
2. When water is bubbling, tenderly put eggs in water and flip using a large spoon.
3. While your eggs are cooking, place one tsp of margarine in a microwave-safe bowl and microwave until dissolved, for around 20 seconds.
4. In the meantime, take the pan and cautiously spill out the excessive water carefully.
5. Cautiously remove shell from every egg, wash to remove any shell parts, and add in the softened margarine.
6. Add the thyme leaves as well as the salt and pepper for flavor.

Nutrition: 159 Calories 18g Fat 8g Protein

132. Fluffy Microwave Scrambled Eggs

Preparation Time: 5 minutes
Cooking Time: 5 minutes
Serving: 2

Ingredients
- 4 eggs
- 1/4 cup milk
- 1/8 teaspoon salt

Direction
1. Break the eggs into a microwavable bowl. Add milk and salt; blend well.
2. Pop the bowl into the microwave and cook on high for 30 seconds. Remove the bowl, beat eggs well overall, scratching down the sides of the bowl, and place back into the microwave for an additional 30 seconds.
3. Repeat this example, blending like clockwork for up to 2 1/2 minutes. Stop when eggs have the consistency you want.

Nutrition: 141 Calories 9.3g Fat 12.3g Protein

133. Caesar Salad Deviled Eggs

Preparation Time: 120 minutes
Cooking Time: 10 minutes
Serving: 4

Ingredients
- 6 large pastured eggs
- 1/3 cup creamy Caesar dressing
- 1/2 cup Parmesan cheese
- Cracked black pepper
- 1 romaine lettuce leaf

Direction
1. In a blending bowl, crush the egg yolks with a fork. Add Caesar dressing, 1/4 cup of the Parmesan cheddar and half of the chopped lettuce, then mix.
2. Utilize a baked good sack to pipe the blend into the egg whites.
3. Top each egg with a little Parmesan cheddar, shredded lettuce and black pepper.

Nutrition: 254 Calories 22g Fat 13.5g Protein

134. Caesar Egg Salad Lettuce Wraps

Preparation Time: 10 minutes
Cooking Time: 10 minutes
Serving: 4

Ingredients
- 6 large hard-boiled eggs
- 3 tbsp. creamy Caesar and 3 tbsp. mayonnaise
- 1/2 cup Parmesan cheese
- Cracked black pepper
- 4 large romaine lettuce leaves

Direction
1. In a blending bowl, mix eggs, velvety Caesar dressing, mayonnaise, 1/4 cup Parmesan cheddar and black pepper.
2. Spoon blend into a mixture of romaine leaves and top with residual Parmesan cheddar.

Nutrition: 254 Calories 22g Fat 13.5g Protein

135. Sour Cream and Chive Egg Clouds

Preparation Time: 10 minutes
Cooking Time: 6 minutes
Serving: 4

Ingredients
- 8 large pastured eggs
- 1/4 cup sharp white cheddar cheese
- 1/4 cup sour cream
- 1 tsp garlic powder
- 2 chives and 2 tsp salted butter

Direction
1. Preheat stove to 450°. Line an oven tray with parchment paper.
2. Separate the eggs, emptying the whites into an enormous blending bowl, and the yolks into singular ramekins.
3. Utilizing an electric blender, whip the egg whites until they are fleecy and solid pinnacles have begun to frame.
4. Utilizing an elastic spatula, delicately overlap in cheddar, cream, garlic powder, and half of the chives.
5. Spoon blend into 8 separate hills on the parchment paper. Make a hole in the focal point of each cloud.
6. Heat for 6 minutes or until the mists are golden on top and the yolks are set.
7. Put a modest quantity of margarine over every yolk. Top with chives.
8. Serve and Enjoy

Nutrition: 117 Calories 10g Fat 6g Protein

136. Turkey and Cheese Rolls

Preparation Time: 15 minutes
Cooking Time: 15 minutes
Serving: 3

Ingredients:
- 6 slices of all-natural turkey breast
- 3 slices all-natural Colby jack cheese

Direction
1. Lay turkey breast level on a plate then lay a portion of the Colby jack over each bit of turkey.
2. Roll.
3. Pack them up in a compartment as quick snacks for work the following day.

Nutrition: 104 Calories 3g Fat 7g Protein

137. Bacon-Wrapped Avocado Fries

Preparation Time: 10 minutes
Cooking Time: 10 minutes
Servings: 20

Ingredients:
- 20 strips of pre-cooked packaged bacon
- 1 large avocado sliced into thin fry-size pieces

Direction
1. Preheat stove to 425°F. Take one strip of precooked bacon and attempt to tenderly stretch somewhat longer without it breaking.
2. Cautiously fold-over avocado, beginning toward one side and attempting to the opposite end.
3. Repeat with remaining ingredients and put onto an oven tray. Heat for 5-10 minutes and serve.

Nutrition: 65 Calories 5.1g Fat 4g Protein

139. Crispy Sweet Potato Fries

Preparation Time: 15 minutes
Cooking Time: 10 minutes
Serving: 4

Ingredients

- 1 1/2 lbs. sweet potatoes
- Sea salt
- Garlic powder
- Onion powder

Direction

1. In a cast-iron skillet over medium-high to high heat, add 1/2 to 1 inch of oil.
2. When the oil is hot and you can begin to see little air pockets forming, add the sweet potato fries to the container.
3. Fry until they are brilliant darker and marginally firm, around 10 minutes.
4. Remove from oil and move to a paper towel to absorb excess oil.
5. Add sea salt, garlic powder and onion powder in a little bowl. Sprinkle flavoring over top of the sweet potato fries.

Nutrition: 102 Calories 8g Fat 4g Protein

140. Baked Eggs and Asparagus with Parmesan

Preparation Time: 7 minutes
Cooking Time: 18 minutes
Serving: 2

Ingredients

- thick asparagus spears
- 4- eggs
- 2- tsp. olive oil
- salt and black pepper
- 2- T Parmesan cheese

Direction

1. Preheat the stove to 400F/200C and shower two gratin dishes with a spray of olive oil.
2. Break each egg into a little dish and give eggs a chance to come to room temperature while you cook the asparagus.
3. Remove the base of every asparagus and dispose of it. Cut the remainder of asparagus into short pieces under 2 inches in length.
4. Put a large portion of the asparagus pieces into each gratin dish and put dishes into the stove to cook the asparagus, setting a clock for 10 minutes.
5. Once the timer goes off, remove gratin dishes from the stove and cautiously slide two eggs over the asparagus in each dish. Set back in the stove and set the clock for 5 minutes.
6. Following 5 minutes, remove gratin dishes and sprinkle each with a tablespoon of coarsely-ground Parmesan.

Nutrition: 248 Calories 19g Fat 20g Protein

141. Cauliflower-Spinach Side Dish

Preparation Time: 10 minutes
Cooking Time: 5 minutes
Serving: 7

Ingredients

- 2 3/4 cups cauliflower florets
- 2 cups spinach leaves
- 2 tablespoons butter
- 1 teaspoon of sea salt
- 2 spreadable cheese wedges

Direction

1. Run cauliflower through a nourishment processor to get 2 cups of shredded cauliflower just bigger than the consistency of cornmeal.
2. Add cauliflower, spinach, margarine, and salt in a huge pot over low heat.
3. Cover and cook until cauliflower is delicate and spinach has withered, 5 to 7 minutes. Mix in cheddar wedges until the cauliflower and spinach are covered and no cheddar bunches remain.

Nutrition: 180 Calories 14g Fat 3.2g Protein

142. Savory Salmon Fat Bombs

Preparation Time: 2 hours
Cooking Time: 0 minute
Serving: 6

Ingredients

- 1/2 cup full-fat cream cheese
- 1/3 cup butter
- 1/2 package smoked salmon
- 1 tbsp fresh lemon juice
- 1-2 tbsp freshly chopped dill

Direction
1. Put the cream cheese, butter and smoked salmon into a nourishment processor.
2. Add lemon juice and dill and beat until smooth.
3. Line a plate with parchment paper and make little fat bombs utilizing around 2 1/2 tablespoons of the blend per piece.
4. Trimming with more dill and put in the cooler for 1-2 hours or until firm

Nutrition: 300 Calories 30g Fat 3g Protein

143. Pistachio Arugula Salad

Preparation Time: 20 minutes
Cooking Time: 0 minutes
Serving: 6

Ingredients:
- 6 Cups Kale, Chopped Rough
- 2 Cups arugula
- ½ Teaspoon Smoked Paprika
- 1/3 Cup Pistachios, Unsalted & Shelled
- 6 Tablespoons Parmesan, Grated

Directions:
1. Get out a large bowl and combine your oil, 2 tbsp. of lemon juice, kale and smoked paprika. Massage it into the leaves for about fifteen seconds. You then need to allow it to sit for ten minutes.
2. Mix everything together before serving with grated cheese on top.

Nutrition: 150 Calories 5g Protein 12g Fat

144. Potato Salad

Preparation Time: 9 minutes
Cooking Time: 12 minutes
Serving: 6
Ingredients:
- 2 lbs. Golden Potatoes, Cubed in 1 Inch Pieces
- ¼ Teaspoon Sea Salt, Fine
- ½ Cup Olives, Sliced
- 1 Cup Celery, Sliced
- 2 Tablespoons Oregano, mint leaves

Directions:
1. Take a medium pot and put your potatoes in cold water. Set it over high heat and bring it to a boil before turning the heat down. You want to turn it down to medium-low. Allow it to cook for twelve to fifteen more minutes. The potatoes should be tender when you pierce them with a fork.
2. Get out a small bowl and whisk your oil, 3 tbsp. lemon juice, 1 tbsp. olive brine and salt together.
3. Drain your potatoes using a colander and transfer it to a serving bowl. Pour in three tablespoons of dressing over your potatoes, and mix well with oregano, and min along with the remaining dressing.

Nutrition: 175 Calories 3g Protein 7g Fat

145. Flavorful Braised Kale

Preparation Time: 9 minutes
Cooking Time: 23 minutes
Serving: 6

Ingredients:
- 1 lb. Kale, Stems Removed & Chopped Roughly
- 1 Cup Cherry Tomatoes, Halved
- 4 Cloves Garlic, Sliced Thin
- ½ Cup Vegetable Stock
- 1 Tablespoon Lemon Juice, Fresh

Directions:
1. Warm up olive oil in a frying pan using medium heat, and add in your garlic. Sauté for a minute or two until lightly golden.
2. Mix your kale and vegetable stock with your garlic, adding it to your pan.
3. Cover the pan and then turn the heat down to medium-low.
4. Allow it to cook until your kale wilts and part of your vegetable stock should be dissolved. It should take roughly five minutes.
5. Stir in your tomatoes and cook without a lid until your kale is tender, and then remove it from heat.
6. Mix in your salt, pepper and lemon juice before serving warm.

Nutrition: 70 Calories 4g Protein 0.5g Fat

147. Bean Salad

Preparation Time: 15 minutes
Cooking Time: 0 minute
Serving: 6

Ingredients:
- 1 Can Garbanzo Beans, Rinsed & Drained
- 1/3 Cup Parsley, Fresh & Chopped
- 1 Red Onion, Diced
- 6 Lettuce Leaves
- ½ Cup Celery, Chopped Fine/Black Pepper to Taste

Directions:
1. Make the vinaigrette dressing by whipping together your 4 garlic cloves, parsley, 2 tbsp. vinegar and pepper in a bowl.
2. Add the olive oil to this mixture and whisk before setting it aside.
3. Add in your onion and beans, and then pour your dressing on top. Toss until it's coated together and then cover it. Chill until it's time to serve.
4. Place a lettuce leaf on the plate when serving and spoon the mixture in. garnish with celery.

Nutrition: 218 Calories 7g Protein 0.4g Fat

148. Basil Tomato Skewers

Preparation Time: 6 minutes
Cooking Time: 0 minute
Serving: 2

Ingredients:
- 16 Mozzarella Balls, Fresh & Small
- 16 Basil Leaves, Fresh
- 16 Cherry Tomatoes
- Olive Oil to Drizzle
- Sea Salt & Black Pepper to Taste

Directions:
1. Start by threading your basil, cheese and tomatoes together on small skewers.
2. Dash with oil before seasoning with salt and pepper. Serve immediately.

Nutrition: 46 Calories 7.6g Protein 0.9g Fat

149. Olives with Feta

Preparation Time: 5 minutes
Cooking Time: 0 minute
Serving: 4

Ingredients:
- ½ Cup Feta Cheese, Diced
- 1 Cup Kalamata Olives, Sliced & Pitted
- 2 Cloves Garlic, Sliced
- 1 Lemon, Zested & Juiced
- 1 Teaspoon Rosemary, Fresh & Chopped

Directions:
1. Mix everything together and serve over crackers.

Nutrition: 71 Calories 4g Protein 2.6g Fat

150. Black Bean Medley

Preparation Time: 5 minutes
Cooking Time: 0 minute
Serving: 4

Ingredients:
- 4 Plum Tomatoes, Chopped
- 14.5 Ounces Black Beans, Canned & Drained
- ½ Red Onion, Sliced
- ¼ Cup Dill, Feta Cheese
- 1 Lemon, Juiced

Directions:
1. Mix everything in a bowl except for your feta and salt. Top the beans with salt and feta.

Nutrition: 121 Calories 6g Protein 5g Fat

151. Grilled Fish with Lemons

Preparation Time: 12 minutes
Cooking Time: 22 minutes
Serving: 4

Ingredients:
- 3-4 Lemons
- 1 Tablespoon Olive Oil
- 4 Catfish Fillets, 4 Ounces Each

Directions:
1. Pat your fillets dry using a paper towel and let them come to room temperature. This may take

ten minutes. Coat the cooking grate of your grill with nonstick cooking spray while it's cold. Once it's coated preheat it to 400 degrees.
2. Cut one lemon in half, setting it to the side. Slice your remaining half of the lemon into ¼ inch slices. Get out a bowl and squeeze a tablespoon of juice from your reserved half. Add your oil to the bowl, mixing well.
3. Brush your fish down with the oil and lemon mixture.
4. Place your lemon slices on the grill and then put our fillets on top. Grill with your lid closed. Turn the fish halfway through if they're more than a half an inch thick.

Nutrition: 147 Calories 22g Protein 1g Fat

152. Lemon Faro Bowl

Preparation Time: 6 minutes
Cooking Time: 20 minutes
Serving: 6

Ingredients:
- 1 Carrot
- 2 Cups Vegetable Broth, Low Sodium
- 1 Cup Onion, Pearled Faro
- 2 Avocados, Peeled, Pitted & Sliced
- 1 Lemon, Small

Directions:
1. Preheat saucepan over medium-high heat. Add in a tablespoon of oil and then throw in your onion once the oil is hot. Cook for about five minutes, stirring frequently to keep it from burning.
2. Add in your carrot and 2 garlic cloves. Allow it to cook for about another minute while you continue to stir.
3. Add in your broth and faro. Let it boil and adjust your heat to high to help. Once it boils, lower it to medium-low and cover your saucepan. Let it simmer for twenty minutes. The faro should be al dente and plump.
4. Pour the faro into a bowl and add in your avocado and zest. Drizzle with your remaining oil and add in your lemon wedges.

Nutrition: 279 Calories 7g Protein 14g Fat

153. Chickpea & Red Pepper Delight

Preparation Time: 26 minutes
Cooking Time: 8 minutes
Serving: 3

Ingredients:
- 1 Red Bell Pepper, Diced
- 2 Cups Water
- ¼ Cup Red Wine Vinegar
- 2 Cloves Garlic, Chopped
- 29 Ounces Chickpeas, Canned, Drained & Rinsed

Directions:
1. In a baking sheet, put your red bell pepper on it with the skin side up.
2. Bake for eight minutes. The skin should bubble, and then place it in a bag to seal it.
3. Remove your bell peppers in about ten minutes, and then slice it into thin slices.
4. Get out two cups of water and pour it in a bowl. Microwave for four minutes and add in 4 sundried tomatoes, letting them sit for ten minutes.
5. Drain them before slicing into thin strips. Mix your red wine vinegar and garlic with your olive oil. Season roasted red bell pepper with parsley, sun dried tomatoes, and chickpeas. Season with salt before serving.

Nutrition: 195 Calories 9.3g Protein 8.5g Fat

154. Pesto Pasta

Preparation Time: 10 minutes
Cooking Time: 0 minute
Serving: 4

Ingredients:
- 3 Cloves Garlic, Minced Fine
- 1/2 Cup Basil Leaves, Fresh
- ¼ Cup Parmesan Cheese Grated
- ¼ Cup Pine Nuts
- 8 Ounces Whole Wheat Pasta

Directions:
1. Start by cooking your pasta per package instructions.
2. In a blender combine all remaining ingredients to make your pesto.
3. Serve with hot pasta.

Nutrition: 405 Calories 13g Protein 21g Fat

155. Eggplant Rolls

Preparation Time: 11 minutes
Cooking Time: 8 minutes
Serving: 6

Ingredients:
- 1 Eggplant, ½ Inch Sliced Lengthwise
- 1/3 Cup Cream Cheese
- ½ Cup Tomatoes, Chopped
- 1 Clove Garlic, Minced
- 2 Tablespoons Dill, Chopped

Directions:
1. Slice your eggplant before brushing it down with olive oil. Sprinkle eggplant slices with salt and pepper.
2. Grill the eggplants for three minutes per side.
3. Get out a bowl and mix cream cheese, garlic, dill and tomatoes in a different bowl.
4. Allow your eggplant slices to cool and then spread the mixture over each one. Roll them and pin them with a toothpick to serve.

Nutrition: 91 Calories 2.1g Protein 7g Fat

156. Heavenly Quinoa

Preparation Time: 7 minutes
Cooking Time: 17 minutes
Serving: 5

Ingredients:
- 1 Cup Almonds, Quinoa
- 1 Teaspoon Vanilla, Cinnamon
- 2 Cups Milk
- 3 Dates, Dried, Pitted & Chopped Fine
- 5 Apricots, Dried & Chopped Fine

Directions:
1. Get out a skillet to toast your almonds in for about five minutes.
2. Place your quinoa and cinnamon in a saucepan using medium heat. Add in your vanilla, salt and milk. Stir and then bring it to a boil. Reduce heat, and allow it to simmer for fifteen minutes.
3. Add in your dates, 2 tbsps. honey, apricots and half of the almonds.
4. Serve topped with almonds and parsley if desired.

Nutrition: 344 Calories 12.6g Protein 13.8g Fat

157. Roasted Squash Bisque

Preparation Time: 13 minutes
Cooking Time: 1 hour
Serving: 2

Ingredients:
- 1 ½ Cups Winter Squash, Chopped
- 1 Clove Garlic, Minced
- 1 Cup Vegetable Broth, Low Sodium
- ¼ Teaspoon Nutmeg
- 1/3 Cup Almond Milk, Unsweetened / ¼ Cup Pistachios, Chopped Fine

Directions:
1. Start by heating your oven to 375F, and then spread your squash on a baking sheet. Bake for forty minutes to one hours. Allow your squash to cool, and then place it in a food processor.
2. Add in your pepper, garlic, nutmeg and broth. Mix until smooth.
3. Pour this soup mixture into a large saucepan and place it over a low heat. Stir constantly until your soup comes to a boil, which should take about five minutes.
4. Stir in your almond milk, and allow it to continue to cook and bubble for about five minutes.
5. Garnish with chopped pistachios before serving.

Nutrition: 244 Calories 6g Protein 13g Fat

158. Red Egg Skillet

Preparation Time: 4 minutes
Cooking Time: 16 minutes
Serving: 6

Ingredients:
- 7 Greek Olives, Pitted & Sliced
- 3 Tomatoes, Ripe & Diced
- 4 Eggs
- ¼ Cup Parsley, Fresh & Chopped
- 1/8 Teaspoon Sea Salt, Fine

Directions:
1. Get out a pan and grease it. Throw your tomatoes in and cook for ten minutes before adding in your olives. Cook for another five minutes.
2. Add your eggs into the pan, cooking over medium-heat so that your eggs are cooked all the way through.
3. Season with salt and pepper and serve topped with parsley.

Nutrition: 188 Calories 10.3g Protein 15.5g Fat

SOUP AND STEWS RECIPES

159. Meatball Soup

Preparation Time: 10 minutes
Cooking Time: 30 minutes
Serving: 4

Ingredients:
- 1 cup ground pork
- ½ teaspoon ground black pepper
- 1 garlic clove, onion
- 1 teaspoon ground thyme
- 3 cups chicken stock

Direction
1. Heat 1 tsp. avocado oil in the saucepan.
2. Add diced onion and cook it for 3 minutes.
3. Meanwhile, mix up ground pork, ground black pepper, minced garlic, and ground thyme.
4. Make the meatballs.
5. Pour the chicken stock in the onion and bring it to boil.
6. Add meatballs and cook the soup for 10 minutes over the medium heat.

Nutrition: 141 calories 22.7g protein 3.8g carbohydrates

160. Soup with Eggs

Preparation Time: 10 minutes
Cooking Time: 10 minutes
Serving: 4

Ingredients:
- 1 onion, diced
- 4 cups chicken stock
- 2 eggs, beaten
- 2 cups snap peas, frozen
- 1 oz Parmesan, grated

Direction
1. Heat a saucepan with 1 tbsp. olive oil over medium-high heat, add onion, stir and cook for 2 minutes.
2. Add stock and bring to a boil.
3. Add eggs and all remaining ingredients in the soup.
4. Cook it for 7 minutes more.

Nutrition: 163 calories 10g protein 14.2g carbohydrates

161. Peas Soup

Preparation Time: 10 minutes
Cooking Time: 25 minutes
Serving: 4

Ingredients:
- ¼ cup long-grain rice
- 4 cups chicken stock
- ½ cup Cheddar cheese, peas
- ¼ teaspoon ground black pepper
- ½ teaspoon Italian seasonings

Direction
1. Heat a saucepan with the stock.
2. Add all ingredients except Cheddar cheese and bring the soup to boil.
3. Then add cheese and stir it well.
4. Cook the soup for 5 minutes over the low heat.

Nutrition: 95 calories 5.4g protein 6.1g carbohydrates

162. Red Lentil Soup

Preparation Time: 5 minutes
Cooking Time: 35 minutes
Serving: 5

Ingredients:
- 8 cups chicken broth
- cup red lentils
- 1 bell pepper, onion
- 1 tablespoon tomato paste
- 1 teaspoon chili powder

Direction:
1. Melt 1 tsp. olive oil in the saucepan and add onion and bell pepper.
2. Roast the vegetables for 5 minutes.
3. After this, add red lentils, tomato paste, chili powder, and chicken broth. Stir the soup well.
4. Cook the soup for 30 minutes over the medium heat.

Nutrition: 225 calories 18.4g protein 29.3g carbohydrates

163. Gazpacho

Preparation Time: 10 minutes
Cooking Time: 0 minute
Serving: 2

Ingredients:
- cup tomatoes
- Kalamata olives, diced
- 1 teaspoon Italian seasonings
- tablespoons olive oil
- 1 cucumber, chopped

Direction:
1. Blend the tomatoes until smooth.
2. Add olives, Italian seasonings, olive oil, and cucumber.
3. Stir the soup.

Nutrition: 171 calories 1.8g protein 9.5g carbohydrates

164. Melon Gazpacho

Preparation Time: 10 minutes
Cooking Time: 0 minute
Serving: 5

Ingredients:
- 1-pound cantaloupe, peeled, chopped
- 1 tablespoon avocado oil
- 1 red onion, diced
- ¼ cup of water
- 1 teaspoon dried basil

Direction
1. Incorporate all ingredients in the blender until smooth.
2. Pour the cooked gazpacho in the serving bowls.

Nutrition: 43 calories 1g protein 9.6g carbohydrates

165. Chicken Soup

Preparation Time: 10 minutes
Cooking Time: 30 minutes
Serving: 6

Ingredients:
- 1-pound chicken breast, skinless, boneless, chopped
- ½ cup fresh parsley, chopped
- ½ teaspoon ground black pepper
- 1 onion, diced
- 6 cups of water

Direction
1. Melt the 1 tsp. olive oil in the pan and add the onion.
2. Cook it until light brown.
3. Add chicken breast, parsley, and ground black pepper.
4. Add water and simmer the soup for 25 minutes.

Nutrition: 102 calories 16.4g protein 2.2g carbohydrates

166. Spicy Tomato Soup

Preparation Time: 10 minutes
Cooking Time: 15 minutes
Serving: 4

Ingredients:
- 2 cups tomatoes, chopped
- 1 cup beef broth
- 1 teaspoon cayenne pepper, basil
- 1 teaspoon ground paprika
- 1 oz Parmesan, grated

Direction
1. Blend the tomatoes and pour the mixture in the saucepan.
2. Add all remaining ingredients except Parmesan and bring the soup to boil.
3. Then ladle the cooked soup in the bowls and top with Parmesan.

Nutrition: 69 calories 5.9g protein 6.1g carbohydrates

167. Chicken Strips Soup

Preparation Time: 5
Cooking Time: 30 minutes
Serving: 4

Ingredients:
- 8 oz. chicken fillet, cut into strips
- 2 tablespoons fresh cilantro, chopped
- 1 cup plain yogurt
- 2 cups of water
- 1 teaspoon chili flakes

Direction
1. Put all ingredients in the pan and simmer for 30 minutes on the low heat.

Nutrition: 152 calories 19.9g protein 4.4g carbohydrates

168. Tomato Bean Soup

Preparation Time: 10 minutes
Cooking Time: 40 minutes
Serving: 4

Ingredients:
- 5 oz. beef tenderloin, sliced
- ½ cup white beans, soaked
- 5 cups of water
- ½ teaspoon chili flakes
- tablespoons tomato paste

Direction:
1. Put all ingredients in the saucepan and stir until tomato paste is dissolved
2. Close the lid and cook the soup for 40 minutes over the medium-low heat.

Nutrition: 332 calories 28.3 g protein 47.2g carbohydrates

169. Zucchini Soup

Preparation Time: 10 minutes
Cooking Time: 10 minutes
Serving: 4

Ingredients:
- 2 zucchinis, spiralized
- 2 tablespoons Greek yogurt
- 1 teaspoon dried oregano
- 3 cups chicken stock
- 2 oz Parmesan, grated

Direction:
1. Pour chicken stock in the pan.
2. Add oregano and Greek yogurt and bring the liquid to boil.
3. Add spiralized zucchini and remove the soup from the heat.
4. Leave it for 10 minutes.
5. After this, add Parmesan and stir the soup gently.

Nutrition: 77 calories 7.3g protein 5g carbohydrates

170. Pasta Soup

Preparation Time: 10 minutes
Cooking Time: 30 minutes
Serving: 4

Ingredients:
- 6 oz chicken breast, skinless, boneless, chopped
- 4 oz whole-grain pasta
- 5 cups of water
- 1 teaspoon white pepper
- ½ teaspoon salt

Direction
1. Pour water in the pan and bring it to boil.
2. Add chicken breast, white pepper, and salt. Simmer the chicken for 15 minutes.
3. Then add pasta and cook the soup for 10 minutes more.

Nutrition: 260 calories 18.1g protein 39.3g carbohydrates

171. White Mushrooms Soup

Preparation Time: 10 minutes
Cooking Time: 25 minutes
Serving: 2

Ingredients:
- 4 oz white mushrooms, chopped
- ¼ cup Cheddar cheese, shredded
- ½ cup white onion, diced
- 1 teaspoon cayenne pepper
- 2 cups of water

Direction
1. Melt the 1 tbsp. olive oil in the pan and add onion and mushrooms.
2. Cook the vegetables for 5 minutes over the medium heat.
3. Then add cayenne pepper and water.
4. Simmer the soup for 10 minutes.
5. Add Cheddar cheese and stir the soup until the cheese is melted.
6. Remove the soup from the heat.

Nutrition: 142 calories 5.7g protein 5.2g carbohydrates

172. Lamb Soup

Preparation Time: 10 minutes
Cooking Time: 35 minutes
Serving: 4

Ingredients:
- 9 oz lamb sirloin, sliced
- 5 cups of water
- 1 cup cauliflower, chopped
- 1 teaspoon dried dill
- 2 tablespoons tomato paste

Direction
1. Preheat the pan well and add lamb sirloin.
2. Roast it for 1 minute per side.
3. Then add water, ½ tsp. ground black pepper, and dried dill.
4. Cook the meat for 20 minutes, covered.
5. Then add tomato paste and cauliflower. Stir the soup.
6. Cook the soup for 10 minutes.

Nutrition: 144 calories 19g protein 3.2g carbohydrates

173. Lemon Zest Soup

Preparation Time: 10 minutes
Cooking Time: 15 minutes
Serving: 2

Ingredients:
- 2 tablespoons lemon juice
- ½ teaspoon lemon zest, grated
- ¼ cup long-grain rice
- 4 cups chicken stock
- 1 celery stalk, chopped

Direction
1. Boil chicken stock then add rice, cook for 10 minutes.
2. Then add lemon zest and celery stalk. Cook the soup for 3 minutes more.
3. After this, add lemon juice and boil it for 2 minutes.

Nutrition: 109 calories 3.2g protein 20.6g carbohydrates

174. Pumpkin Soup

Preparation Time: 30 minutes
Cooking Time: 8 minutes
Serving: 4

Ingredients:
- 1 onion, chopped
- 2 cups sweet potato, chopped
- 30 oz. pumpkin puree
- 1-quart chicken stock
- 1 teaspoon garlic powder

Direction:
1. Add all the ingredients in the Instant Pot.
2. Seal the pot.
3. Press manual button.
4. Cook at high pressure for 8 minutes.
5. Release the pressure quickly.
6. Transfer the contents into a blender.
7. Pulse until smooth.
8. Season with salt and pepper.

Nutrition: 186 Calories 1.4g Fat 10.2g Fiber

175. Lentil Soup

Preparation Time: 8 minutes
Cooking Time: 13 minutes
Serving: 2

Ingredients:
- 1 onion, chopped
- 2 cloves garlic, chopped
- Dried herb mixture: 1/2 teaspoon of each (cumin, coriander, sumac, parsley, mint)
- 1/2 cup red lentils
- 3 cups vegetable broth

Direction:
1. Select the sauté setting in the Instant Pot.
2. Add 2 tablespoons olive oil.
3. Sauté onion for 3 minutes.
4. Add the garlic and dried herb mixture.
5. Cook for 2 minutes, stirring frequently.
6. Add the lentils and broth.
7. Season with salt and pepper.
8. Seal the pot.
9. Choose manual mode.
10. Cook at high pressure for 8 minutes.
11. Release the pressure quickly.

Nutrition: 254 Calories 2.6g Fat 20.5g Protein

176. Chickpea Soup

Preparation Time: 16 minutes
Cooking Time: 22 minutes
Serving: 6

Ingredients:
- 2 cups dry chickpeas, soaked in a bowl of water overnight
- 1 onion, chopped
- 2 carrots, chopped
- 4 teaspoons dried herb mixture (coriander, cumin, pepper, turmeric and all spice)
- 6 cups vegetable broth

Direction:
1. Drain the chickpeas and set aside.
2. Set the Instant Pot to sauté.
3. Add 2 tablespoons olive oil.
4. Add the onion and carrots.
5. Season with salt.
6. Cook for 5 minutes, stirring frequently.
7. Add the chickpeas and broth.
8. Lock the lid in place.
9. Cook at high pressure for 15 minutes.
10. Release the pressure quickly.

Nutrition: 297 Calories 5.4g Fat 45g Carbohydrate

177. Chicken & Tomato Soup

Preparation Time: 30 minutes
Cooking Time: 6 minutes
Serving: 6

Ingredients:
- 3 cloves garlic, minced
- 1 lb. chicken breasts, cubed
- 28 oz. canned crushed tomatoes
- 6 cups chicken broth
- 1 teaspoon mixed garlic and onion powder

Direction:
1. Set the Instant Pot to sauté.
2. Add 1 tablespoon olive oil.
3. Cook the garlic until fragrant.
4. Add the chicken breast cubes.
5. Cook until brown on both sides.
6. Pour in the rest of the ingredients.
7. Seal the pot.
8. Set it to manual mode.
9. Cook at high pressure for 10 minutes.
10. Release the pressure quickly.

Nutrition: 237 Calories 7g Fat 12g Carbohydrate

178. Chicken & Quinoa Stew

Preparation Time: 9 minutes
Cooking Time: 23 minutes
Serving: 6

Ingredients:
- 1 1/4 lb. chicken thigh fillet, sliced into strips
- 4 cups butternut squash, chopped
- 4 cups chicken stock
- 1 cup onion, chopped
- ½ cup uncooked quinoa

Direction:
1. Put the chicken in the Instant Pot.
2. Mix in rest of the ingredients except the quinoa.
3. Cover the pot.
4. Turn it to manual.
5. Cook at high pressure for 8 minutes.
6. Release the pressure naturally.
7. Stir the quinoa into the stew.
8. Set it to sauté.
9. Cook for 15 minutes.

Nutrition: 251 Calories 4.2g Fat 22g Carbohydrate

179. Vegetable & Lentil Soup

Preparation Time: 13 minutes
Cooking Time: 18 minutes
Serving:

Ingredients:
- 6 cloves garlic, minced
- 4 cups mixed vegetables (cabbage, carrots, bell pepper, potatoes), chopped
- 5 tablespoons mixed spices (cumin, coriander, curry powder, turmeric, all spice)
- 6 cups chicken stock
- 1 1/4 cup green lentils

Direction:
1. Fill in 2 tablespoons olive oil into the Instant Pot.
2. Cook the garlic for 2 minutes.
3. Add the vegetables and spices.
4. Season with salt.
5. Cook for 5 minutes.
6. Pour in the stock and add the lentils.
7. Seal the pot.
8. Choose manual mode.
9. Cook at high pressure for 12 minutes.
10. Release the pressure naturally.

Nutrition: 257 Calories 1.7g Fat 44.9g Carbohydrate

181. Carrot Soup

Preparation Time: 27 minutes
Cooking Time: 7 minutes
Serving: 3

Ingredients:
- 1 onion, chopped
- 1 lb. carrots, cubed
- 1/4 teaspoon cumin powder
- 1/4 teaspoon smoked paprika
- 3 cups vegetable broth

Direction:
1. Choose the sauté setting in the Instant Pot.
2. Pour in 2 tablespoons olive oil.
3. Cook onion for 2 minutes.
4. Add the rest of the ingredients.
5. Secure the lid.
6. Hit manual button.
7. Cook at high pressure for 5 minutes.
8. Release the pressure naturally.
9. Transfer the contents to a blender.
10. Blend until smooth.
11. Season with salt and pepper.

Nutrition: 116 Calories 1.5g Fat 6.6g Protein

182. Lentil & Spinach Soup

Preparation time: 20 minutes
Cooking Time: 16 minutes
Serving: 4

Ingredients:
- 1 cup onion, diced
- 4 teaspoons spice mixture (cumin, turmeric, thyme)
- 1 cup dry brown lentils
- 4 cups vegetable broth
- 6 cups baby spinach

Direction:
1. Choose the sauté function in the Instant Pot.
2. Pour in 1 tablespoon of olive oil.
3. Cook the onion for 2 minutes.
4. Add the spice mixture.
5. Season with salt and pepper.
6. Add the lentils and broth.
7. Secure the lid.
8. Select manual setting.
9. Cook at high pressure for 12 minutes.
10. Release the pressure quickly.
11. Mix in the spinach and wait for it to wilt.
12. Season with salt and pepper.

Nutrition: 230 Calories 2.1g Fat 19g Protein

183. Greek Veggie Soup

Preparation Time: 19 minutes
Cooking Time: 17 minutes
Serving: 4

Ingredients:
- 1 clove garlic, minced
- 3 cups cabbage, shredded
- 2 carrots, minced
- 4 cups vegetable broth
- 15 oz. canned roasted tomatoes

Direction:
1. Stir in 2 tablespoons of olive oil into the Instant Pot.
2. Add the garlic and cabbage.
3. Cook for 5 minutes.
4. Add the carrots and cook for 2 more minutes.
5. Pour in the broth and tomatoes.
6. Season with salt and pepper.
7. Seal the pot.
8. Set it to soup mode and adjust time to 10 minutes.
9. Release the pressure naturally.

Nutrition: 94 Calories 1.4g Fat 6.8g Protein

185. Veggie Stew

Preparation Time: 19 minutes
Cooking Time: 23 minutes
Serving: 4

Ingredients:
- 1 onion, minced
- 1 package mixed frozen vegetables (carrots, potatoes, beans, broccoli)
- 4 cups vegetable broth
- 20 oz. tomato sauce
- 2 tsp. Italian seasoning

Direction:
1. Set the Instant Pot to sauté.
2. Add 1 tablespoon of olive oil.
3. Cook the onion for 1 minute.
4. Add the frozen vegetables.
5. Cook for 3 to 5 minutes.
6. Add the rest of the ingredients.
7. Cover the pot and set it to manual.
8. Cook at high pressure for 15 minutes.
9. Release the pressure naturally.
10. Season with salt and pepper.

Nutrition: 138 Calories 2.5g Fat 8.7g Protein

186. Carrot & Mushroom Soup

Preparation Time: 17 minutes
Cooking Time: 16 minutes
Serving: 4

Ingredients:
- 1 onion, diced
- 2 stalks celery, sliced
- 2 carrots, sliced
- 1/4 cup mushroom
- 4 cups chicken stock

Direction:
1. Stir in 1 tablespoon olive oil to the pot.
2. Cook the onion, celery, carrots and mushroom for 5 minutes.
3. Cover the pot.
4. Choose manual function.
5. Pour in the stock.
6. Close the pot.
7. Select manual mode.
8. Cook at high pressure for 10 minutes.
9. Release the pressure naturally.

Nutrition: 71 Calories 1.2g Fat 2.9g Protein

187. White Bean & Swiss Chard Stew

Preparation Time: 17 minutes
Cooking Time: 4 minutes
Serving: 8

Ingredients:
- 1 lb. dried Great Northern beans, rinsed and soaked overnight
- 2 teaspoons dried herbs (rosemary, oregano)
- 28 oz. canned roasted tomatoes
- 1 bunch Swiss chard, chopped into ribbons
- 4 cups vegetable stock

Direction:
1. Pour 1 tablespoon olive oil into the Instant Pot.
2. Add the beans, dried herbs and tomatoes.
3. Season with salt and pepper.
4. Cook for 1 minute.
5. Pour in the broth.
6. Seal the pot.
7. Choose bean/chili function.
8. Release the pressure quickly.
9. Select the sauté button.
10. Add the Swiss chard and cook for 3 minutes.

Nutrition: 241 Calories 0.8g Fat 15g Protein

188. White Bean & Kale Soup

Preparation Time: 18 minutes
Cooking Time: 13 minutes
Serving: 10

Ingredients:
- 1 white onion, chopped
- 4 cups vegetable stock
- 28 oz. canned diced tomatoes
- 30 oz. white cannellini beans
- 4 cups kale

Direction:
1. Pour 3 tablespoons olive oil to the Instant Pot.
2. Sauté the white onion for 3 minutes.
3. Add the rest of the ingredients.
4. Switch it to manual setting.
5. Cover the pot and cook at high pressure for 10 minutes.
6. Release the pressure naturally.
7. Stir in the kale.
8. Cover the pot and wait for the kale to wilt before serving.

Nutrition: 206 Calories 0.5g Fat 12.5g Protein

189. Bacon & Potato Soup

Preparation Time: 36 minutes
Cooking Time: 12 minutes
Serving: 6

Ingredients:
- 4 slices bacon, sliced in half
- 1/2 cup onion, chopped
- 1 1/2 lb. potatoes, diced
- 2 cups chicken stock
- 1/2 cup sour cream

Direction:
1. Pour 1 tablespoon olive oil into the Instant Pot.
2. Add the bacon and cook until crispy.
3. Drain in paper towel and then chop.
4. Add the onion and cook for 2 minutes.
5. Add the potatoes and stock.
6. Cover the pot.
7. Set it to manual.
8. Cook at high pressure for 10 minutes.
9. Release the pressure naturally.
10. Transfer the contents to a blender.
11. Puree until smooth.
12. Stir in the sour cream.
13. Top with the crispy bacon bits.

Nutrition: 195 Calories 9.6g Fat 7.6g Protein

190. Lemon Chicken Soup

Preparation time: 18 minutes
Cooking Time: 11 minutes
Serving: 4

Ingredients:
- 3 chicken breast fillets
- 1 onion, diced
- 1 teaspoon garlic powder
- 2 tablespoons lemon juice
- 6 cups chicken stock

Direction:
1. Situate all the ingredients except the lemon juice in the Instant Pot.
2. Mix well.
3. Choose manual setting.
4. Cook at high pressure for 10 minutes.
5. Release the pressure naturally.
6. Remove the chicken and shred.
7. Put it back to the pot and press sauté.
8. Stir in the lemon juice.
9. Season with salt and pepper.

Nutrition: 238 Calories 9.1g Fat 33g Protein

VEGETARIAN RECIPES

191. Mediterranean Veggie Bowl

Preparation Time: 10 minutes
Cooking Time: 20 minutes
Serving: 4

Ingredients:
- 1 cup quinoa, rinsed
- 1½ teaspoons salt, divided
- 2 cups cherry tomatoes, cut in half
- 1 large bell pepper, cucumber
- 1 cup Kalamata olives

Direction
1. Using medium pot over medium heat, boil 2 cups of water. Add the bulgur (or quinoa) and 1 teaspoon of salt. Cover and cook for 15 to 20 minutes.
2. To arrange the veggies in your 4 bowls, visually divide each bowl into 5 sections. Place the cooked bulgur in one section. Follow with the tomatoes, bell pepper, cucumbers, and olives.
3. Scourge ½ cup of lemon juice, olive oil, remaining ½ teaspoon salt, and black pepper.
4. Evenly spoon the dressing over the 4 bowls.
5. Serve immediately or cover and refrigerate for later.

Nutrition: 772 Calories 6g Protein 41g Carbohydrates

192. Grilled Veggie and Hummus Wrap

Preparation Time: 15 minutes
Cooking Time: 10 minutes
Serving: 6

Ingredients:
- 1 large eggplant
- 1 large onion
- ½ cup extra-virgin olive oil
- 6 lavash wraps or large pita bread
- 1 cup Creamy Traditional Hummus

Direction:
1. Preheat a grill, large grill pan, or lightly oiled large skillet on medium heat.
2. Slice the eggplant and onion into circles. Rub the vegetables with olive oil and sprinkle with salt.
3. Cook the vegetables on both sides, about 3 to 4 minutes each side.
4. To make the wrap, lay the lavash or pita flat. Spread about 2 tablespoons of hummus on the wrap.
5. Evenly divide the vegetables among the wraps, layering them along one side of the wrap. Gently fold over the side of the wrap with the vegetables, tucking them in and making a tight wrap.
6. Lay the wrap seam side-down and cut in half or thirds.
7. You can also wrap each sandwich with plastic wrap to help it hold its shape and eat it later.

Nutrition: 362 Calories 15g Protein 28g Carbohydrates

193. Spanish Green Beans

Preparation Time: 10 minutes
Cooking Time: 20 minutes
Serving: 4

Ingredients:
- 1 large onion, chopped
- 4 cloves garlic, finely chopped
- 1-pound green beans, fresh or frozen, trimmed
- 1 (15-ounce) can diced tomatoes

Direction
1. In a huge pot over medium heat, cook olive oil, onion, and garlic; cook for 1 minute.
2. Cut the green beans into 2-inch pieces.
3. Add the green beans and 1 teaspoon of salt to the pot and toss everything together; cook for 3 minutes.
4. Add the diced tomatoes, remaining ½ teaspoon of salt, and black pepper to the pot; continue to cook for another 12 minutes, stirring occasionally.
5. Serve warm.

Nutrition: 200 Calories 4g Protein 18g Carbohydrates

194. Rustic Cauliflower and Carrot Hash

Preparation Time: 10 minutes
Cooking Time: 10 minutes
Serving: 4

Ingredients:
- 1 large onion, chopped
- 1 tablespoon garlic, minced
- 2 cups carrots, diced
- 4 cups cauliflower pieces, washed
- ½ teaspoon ground cumin

Direction
1. In a big skillet over medium heat, heat up 3 tbsps. of olive oil, onion, garlic, and carrots for 3 minutes.
2. Cut the cauliflower into 1-inch or bite-size pieces. Add the cauliflower, salt, and cumin to the skillet and toss to combine with the carrots and onions.
3. Cover and cook for 3 minutes.
4. Throw the vegetables and continue to cook uncovered for an additional 3 to 4 minutes.
5. Serve warm.

Nutrition: 159 Calories 3g Protein 15g Carbohydrates

195. Roasted Cauliflower and Tomatoes

Preparation Time: 5 minutes
Cooking Time: 25 minutes
Serving: 4

Ingredients:
- 4 cups cauliflower, cut into 1-inch pieces
- 6 tablespoons extra-virgin olive oil, divided
- 4 cups cherry tomatoes
- ½ teaspoon freshly ground black pepper
- ½ cup grated Parmesan cheese

Direction
1. Preheat the oven to 425°F.
2. Add the cauliflower, 3 tablespoons of olive oil, and ½ teaspoon of salt to a large bowl and toss to evenly coat. Pour onto a baking sheet and spread the cauliflower out in an even layer.
3. In another large bowl, add the tomatoes, remaining 3 tablespoons of olive oil, and ½ teaspoon of salt, and toss to coat evenly. Pour onto a different baking sheet.
4. Put the sheet of cauliflower and the sheet of tomatoes in the oven to roast for 17 to 20 minutes until the cauliflower is lightly browned and tomatoes are plump.
5. Using a spatula, spoon the cauliflower into a serving dish, and top with tomatoes, black pepper, and Parmesan cheese. Serve warm.

Nutrition: 294 Calories 9g Protein 13g Carbohydrates

196. Roasted Acorn Squash

Preparation Time: 10 minutes
Cooking Time: 35 minutes
Serving: 6

Ingredients:
- 2 acorn squash, medium to large
- 2 tablespoons extra-virgin olive oil
- 5 tablespoons unsalted butter
- ¼ cup chopped sage leaves
- 2 tablespoons fresh thyme leaves

Direction
1. Preheat the oven to 400°F.
2. Cut the acorn squash in half lengthwise. Scoop out the seeds and cut it horizontally into ¾-inch-thick slices.
3. In a large bowl, drizzle the squash with the olive oil, sprinkle with salt, and toss together to coat.
4. Lay the acorn squash flat on a baking sheet.
5. Put the baking sheet in the oven and bake the squash for 20 minutes. Flip squash over with a spatula and bake for another 15 minutes.
6. Melt the butter in a medium saucepan over medium heat.
7. Add the sage and thyme to the melted butter and let them cook for 30 seconds.
8. Transfer the cooked squash slices to a plate. Spoon the butter/herb mixture over the squash. Season with salt and black pepper. Serve warm.

Nutrition: 188 Calories 1g Protein 16g Carbohydrates

198. Sautéed Garlic Spinach

Preparation Time: 5 minutes
Cooking Time: 10 minutes
Serving: 4

Ingredients:
- ¼ cup extra-virgin olive oil
- 1 large onion, thinly sliced
- 3 cloves garlic, minced
- 6 (1-pound) bags of baby spinach, washed
- 1 lemon, cut into wedges

Directions
1. Cook the olive oil, onion, and garlic in a large skillet for 2 minutes over medium heat.
2. Add one bag of spinach and ½ teaspoon of salt. Cover the skillet and let the spinach wilt for 30 seconds. Repeat (omitting the salt), adding 1 bag of spinach at a time.
3. Once all the spinach has been added, remove the cover and cook for 3 minutes, letting some of the moisture evaporate.
4. Serve warm with lemon juice over the top.

Nutrition: 301 Calories 17g Protein 29g Carbohydrates

199. Garlicky Sautéed Zucchini with Mint

Preparation Time: 5 minutes
Cooking Time: 10 minutes
Serving: 4

Ingredients:
- 3 large green zucchinis
- 3 tablespoons extra-virgin olive oil
- 1 large onion, chopped
- 3 cloves garlic, minced
- 1 teaspoon dried mint

Direction
1. Cut the zucchini into ½-inch cubes.
2. Using huge skillet, place over medium heat, cook the olive oil, onions, and garlic for 3 minutes, stirring constantly.
3. Add the zucchini and salt to the skillet and toss to combine with the onions and garlic, cooking for 5 minutes.
4. Add the mint to the skillet, tossing to combine. Cook for another 2 minutes. Serve warm.

Nutrition: 147 Calories 4g Protein 12g Carbohydrates

200. Stewed Okra

Preparation Time: 5 minutes
Cooking Time: 25 minutes
Serving: 4

Ingredients:
- 4 cloves garlic, finely chopped
- 1 pound fresh or frozen okra, cleaned
- 1 (15-ounce) can plain tomato sauce
- 2 cups water
- ½ cup fresh cilantro, finely chopped

Direction
1. In a big pot at medium heat, stir and cook ¼ cup of olive oil, 1 onion, garlic, and salt for 1 minute.
2. Stir in the okra and cook for 3 minutes.
3. Add the tomato sauce, water, cilantro, and black pepper; stir, cover, and let cook for 15 minutes, stirring occasionally.
4. Serve warm.

Nutrition: 201 Calories 4g Protein 18g Carbohydrates

201. Sweet Veggie-Stuffed Peppers

Preparation Time: 20 minutes
Cooking Time: 30 minutes
Serving: 6

Ingredients:
- 6 large bell peppers, different colors
- 3 cloves garlic, minced
- 1 carrot, chopped
- 1 (16-ounce) can garbanzo beans
- 3 cups cooked rice

Direction
1. Preheat the oven to 350°F.
2. Make sure to choose peppers that can stand upright. Cut off the pepper cap and remove the seeds, reserving the cap for later. Stand the peppers in a baking dish.
3. In a skillet over medium heat, cook up olive oil, 1 onion, garlic, and carrots for 3 minutes.
4. Stir in the garbanzo beans. Cook for another 3 minutes.

5. Remove the pan from the heat and spoon the cooked ingredients to a large bowl.
6. Add the rice, salt, and pepper; toss to combine.
7. Stuff each pepper to the top and then put the pepper caps back on.
8. Cover the baking dish with aluminum foil and bake for 25 minutes.
9. Remove the foil and bake for another 5 minutes.
10. Serve warm.

Nutrition: 301 Calories 8g Protein 50g Carbohydrates

202. **Vegetable-Stuffed Grape Leaves**

Preparation Time: 50 minutes
Cooking Time: 45 minutes
Serving: 7

Ingredients:
- 2 cups white rice, rinsed
- 2 large tomatoes, finely diced
- 1 (16-ounce) jar grape leaves
- 1 cup lemon juice
- 4 to 6 cups water

Direction
1. Incorporate rice, tomatoes, 1 onion, 1 green onion, 1 cup of parsley, 3 garlic cloves, salt, and black pepper.
2. Drain and rinse the grape leaves.
3. Prepare a large pot by placing a layer of grape leaves on the bottom. Lay each leaf flat and trim off any stems.
4. Place 2 tablespoons of the rice mixture at the base of each leaf. Fold over the sides, then roll as tight as possible. Place the rolled grape leaves in the pot, lining up each rolled grape leaf. Continue to layer in the rolled grape leaves.
5. Gently pour the lemon juice and olive oil over the grape leaves, and add enough water to just cover the grape leaves by 1 inch.
6. Lay a heavy plate that is smaller than the opening of the pot upside down over the grape leaves. Cover the pot and cook the leaves over medium-low heat for 45 minutes. Let stand for 20 minutes before serving.
7. Serve warm or cold.

Nutrition: 532 Calories 12g Protein 80g Carbohydrates

203. **Grilled Eggplant Rolls**

Preparation Time: 30 minutes
Cooking Time: 10 minutes
Serving: 5

Ingredients:
- 2 large eggplants
- 4 ounces goat cheese
- 1 cup ricotta
- ¼ cup fresh basil, finely chopped

Direction:
1. Slice the tops of the eggplants off and cut the eggplants lengthwise into ¼-inch-thick slices. Sprinkle the slices with the salt and place the eggplant in a colander for 15 to 20 minutes. The salt will draw out excess water from the eggplant.
2. In a large bowl, combine the goat cheese, ricotta, basil, and pepper.
3. Preheat a grill, grill pan, or lightly oiled skillet on medium heat. Pat the eggplant slices dry using paper towel and lightly spray with olive oil spray. Place the eggplant on the grill, grill pan, or skillet and cook for 3 minutes on each side.
4. Remove the eggplant from the heat and let cool for 5 minutes.
5. To roll, lay one eggplant slice flat, place a tablespoon of the cheese mixture at the base of the slice, and roll up. Serve immediately or chill until serving.

Nutrition: 255 Calories 15g Protein 19g Carbohydrates

204. **Crispy Zucchini Fritters**

Preparation Time: 15 minutes
Cooking Time: 20 minutes
Serving: 6

Ingredients:
- 2 large green zucchinis
- 1 cup flour
- 1 large egg, beaten
- ½ cup water
- 1 teaspoon baking powder

Direction
1. Grate the zucchini into a large bowl.
2. Add the 2 tbsps. of parsley, 3 garlic cloves, salt, flour, egg, water, and baking powder to the bowl and stir to combine.

3. In a large pot or fryer over medium heat, heat oil to 365°F.
4. Drop the fritter batter into 3 cups of vegetable oil. Turn the fritters over using a slotted spoon and fry until they are golden brown, about 2 to 3 minutes.
5. Strain fritters from the oil and place on a plate lined with paper towels.
6. Serve warm with Creamy Tzatziki or Creamy Traditional Hummus as a dip.

Nutrition: 446 Calories 5g Protein 19g Carbohydrates

205. Cheesy Spinach Pies

Preparation Time: 20 minutes
Cooking Time: 40 minutes
Serving: 5

Ingredients:

- 2 tablespoons extra-virgin olive oil
- 3 (1-pound) bags of baby spinach, washed
- 1 cup feta cheese
- 1 large egg, beaten
- Puff pastry sheets

Direction
1. Preheat the oven to 375°F.
2. In a large skillet over medium heat, cook the olive oil, 1 onion, and 2 garlic cloves for 3 minutes.
3. Add the spinach to the skillet one bag at a time, letting it wilt in between each bag. Toss using tongs. Cook for 4 minutes. Once the spinach is cooked, drain any excess liquid from the pan.
4. Mix feta cheese, egg, and cooked spinach.
5. Lay the puff pastry flat on a counter. Cut the pastry into 3-inch squares.
6. Place a tablespoon of the spinach mixture in the center of a puff-pastry square. Fold over one corner of the square to the diagonal corner, forming a triangle. Crimp the edges of the pie by pressing down with the tines of a fork to seal them together. Repeat until all squares are filled.
7. Situate the pies on a parchment-lined baking sheet and bake for 25 to 30 minutes or until golden brown. Serve warm or at room temperature.

Nutrition: 503 Calories 16g Protein 38g Carbohydrates

206. Instant Pot Black Eyed Peas

Preparation Time: 6 minutes
Cooking Time: 25 minutes
Servings: 4

Ingredients

- 2 cups black-eyed peas (dried)
- 1 cup parsley, dill
- 2 slices oranges, 2 tbsp. tomato paste
- 4 green onions
- 2 carrots, bay leaves

Direction
1. Clean the dill thoroughly with water removing stones.
2. Add all the ingredients in the instant pot and stir well to combine.
3. Lid the instant pot and set the vent to sealing.
4. Set time for twenty-five minutes. When the time has elapsed release pressure naturally.
5. Serve and enjoy the black-eyed peas.

Nutrition: 506 Calories 14g Protein 33g Carbohydrates

207. Green Beans and Potatoes in Olive Oil

Preparation Time: 12 minutes
Cooking Time: 17 minutes
Serving: 4

Ingredients

- 15 oz. tomatoes (diced)
- 2 potatoes
- 1 lb. green beans (fresh)
- 1 bunch dill, parsley, zucchini
- 1 tbsp. dried oregano

Direction
1. Turn on the sauté function on your instant pot.
2. Pour tomatoes, a cup of water and olive oil. Add the rest of the ingredients and stir through.
3. Lid the instant pot and set the valve to seal. Set time for fifteen minutes.
4. When the time has elapsed release pressure. Remove the Fasolakia from the instant pot. Serve and enjoy.

Nutrition: 510 Calories 20g Protein 28g Carbohydrates

208. Nutritious Vegan Cabbage

Preparation Time: 35 minutes
Cooking Time: 15 minutes
Serving: 6

Ingredients
- 3 cups green cabbage
- 1 can tomatoes, onion
- Cups vegetable broth
- 3 stalks celery, carrots
- 2 tbsp. vinegar, sage

Direction
1. Mix 1 tbsp. of lemon juice. 2 garlic cloves and the rest of ingredients in the instant pot and. Lid and set time for fifteen minutes on high pressure.
2. Release pressure naturally then remove the lid. Remove the soup from the instant pot.
3. Serve and enjoy.

Nutrition: 67 Calories 0.4g Fat 3.8g Fiber

209. Instant Pot Horta and Potatoes

Preparation Time: 12 minutes
Cooking Time: 17 minutes
Serving: 4

Ingredients
- 2 heads of washed and chopped greens (spinach, Dandelion, kale, mustard green, Swiss chard)
- 6 potatoes (washed and cut in pieces)
- 1 cup virgin olive oil
- 1 lemon juice (reserve slices for serving)
- 10 garlic cloves (chopped)

Direction
1. Position all the ingredients in the instant pot and lid setting the vent to sealing.
2. Set time for fifteen minutes. When time is done release pressure.
3. Let the potatoes rest for some time. Serve and enjoy with lemon slices.

Nutrition: 499 Calories 18g Protein 41g Carbohydrates

210. Instant Pot Jackfruit Curry

Preparation Time: 1 hour
Cooking Time: 16 minutes
Serving: 2

Ingredients
- 1 tbsp. oil
- Cumin seeds, Mustard seeds
- 2 tomatoes (purred)
- 20 oz. can green jackfruit (drained and rinsed)
- 1 tbsp. coriander powder, turmeric.

Direction
1. Turn the instant pot to sauté mode. Add cumin and mustard seeds, and allow them to sizzle.
2. Add other ingredients, and a cup of water then lid the instant pot. Set time for seven minutes on high pressure.
3. When the time has elapsed release pressure naturally, shred the jackfruit and serve.

Nutrition: 369 Calories 3g Fat 6g Fiber

211. Instant Pot Collard Greens with Tomatoes

Preparation Time: 18 minutes
Cooking Time: 8 minutes
Serving: 4

Ingredients
- 1 white onion (diced)
- 3tbsp olive oil
- 3 garlic cloves (minced)
- Cup tomatoes (sun-dried and chopped)
- 1 bunch collard greens (roughly cut and hard stems removed)

Direction
1. Turn on the sauté function on your instant pot.
2. Add onions and olive oil to the instant pot and let cook for three minutes or until lightly browned.
3. Add the rest of ingredients one at a time while stirring.
4. Add salt and pepper to taste and a cup of water. Turn off the sauté function and set to manual. Set time for five minutes at high pressure.
5. When the time has elapsed, release pressure naturally.
6. Open the lid and drizzle a half lemon juice.
7. Serve and enjoy.

Nutrition: 498 Calories 19g Protein 32g Carbohydrates

212. Instant Pot Artichokes with Mediterranean Aioli

Preparation Time: 7 minutes
Cooking Time: 10 minutes
Serving: 3

Ingredients
- 3 medium artichokes (stems cut off)
- 1 cup vegetable broth
- Mediterranean aioli

Direction
1. Place wire trivet in place in the instant pot then place the artichokes on the wire.
2. Pour vegetable broth over artichokes.
3. Lid the instant pot and put steam mode on. Set timer for 10 minutes. When the time has elapsed allow pressure to release.
4. Remove the artichokes from the instant pot and reserve the remaining broth, about a quarter cup.
5. Half the artichokes and place them on serving bowls. Drizzle broth.
6. Serve with aioli and enjoy.

Nutrition: 30 Calories 0.1g Fat 3.5g Fiber

213. Instant Pot Millet Pilaf

Preparation Time: 23 minutes
Cooking Time: 11 minutes
Serving: 4

Ingredients
- 1 cup millet
- Cup apricot and shelled pistachios (roughly chopped)
- 1 lemon juice and zest
- tbsp olive oil
- Cup parsley (fresh)

Direction
1. Pour one and three-quarter cup of water in your instant pot. Place the millet and lid the instant pot.
2. Adjust time for 10 minutes on high pressure. When the time has elapsed, release pressure naturally.
3. Remove the lid and add all other ingredients. Stir while adjusting the seasonings.
4. Serve and enjoy

Nutrition: 308 Calories 11g Fat 6g Fiber

214. Instant Pot Stuffed Sweet Potatoes

Preparation Time: 13 minutes
Cooking Time: 22 minutes
Serving: 2

Ingredients
- 2 sweet potatoes (washed thoroughly)
- cup chickpeas, onions
- 2 spring onions
- 1 avocado
- cooked couscous

Direction
1. Pour a cup and half of water in your instant pot then place steam rack in place.
2. Place the sweet potatoes on the rack. Set the valve to sealing and time for seventeen minutes under high pressure.
3. Meanwhile, roast the chickpeas on your pan with olive oil.
4. Add salt and pepper to taste then paprika. Stir until chickpeas are coated evenly.
5. Cook for a minute then put off the heat.
6. When the instant pot time elapses, release pressure naturally for five minutes. Let the sweet potatoes cool then remove them from the instant pot.
7. Cut the sweet potatoes lengthwise and use a fork to mash the inside creating a space for toppings.
8. Add the pre-prepared toppings then serve with feta cheese lemon wedges.

Nutrition: 776 Calories 26g Fat 23g Protein

216. Instant Pot Couscous and Vegetable Medley

Preparation Time: 9 minutes
Cooking Time: 17 minutes
Serving: 3

Ingredients
- Onion (chopped)
- 1 red bell pepper and carrot (chopped)
- 1 cup couscous Israeli,
- Garam masala, cilantro, lemon juice,
- 2 bays leave

Direction

1. Put on sauté function on your instant pot then add olive oil.
2. Add bay leaves followed by chopped onions the sauté for two minutes.
3. Add pepper and carrots then continue to sauté for one more minute.
4. Stir in couscous, Garam masala, salt to taste and a cup and three-quarter of water.
5. Switch the sauté function to manual and set for two minutes. When the time has elapsed naturally release pressure for ten minutes.
6. Fluff the couscous then mix in lemon juice and garnish with cilantro.
7. Remove from instant pot and serve when hot

Nutrition: 460 Calories 5g Fat 13g Protein

DESSERT RECIPES

217. Chocolate Ganache

Preparation Time: 10 minutes
Cooking Time: 3 minutes
Servings: 16

Ingredients
- 9 ounces bittersweet chocolate, chopped
- cup heavy cream
- 1 tablespoon dark rum (optional)

Direction
1. Put the chocolate in a medium bowl. Heat the cream in a small saucepan over medium heat.
2. Bring to a boil. When the cream has reached a boiling point, pour the chopped chocolate over it and beat until smooth. Stir the rum if desired.
3. Allow the ganache to cool slightly before you pour it on a cake. Begin in the middle of the cake and work outside. For a fluffy icing or chocolate filling, let it cool until thick and beat with a whisk until light and fluffy.

Nutrition: 142 calories 10.8g fat 1.4g protein

218. Chocolate Covered Strawberries

Preparation Time: 15 minutes
Cooking Time: 4 minutes
Servings: 24

Ingredients
- 16 ounces milk chocolate chips
- 2 tablespoons shortening
- 1-pound fresh strawberries with leaves

Direction
1. In a bain-marie, melt chocolate and shortening, occasionally stirring until smooth. Pierce the tops of the strawberries with toothpicks and immerse them in the chocolate mixture.
2. Turn the strawberries and put the toothpick in Styrofoam so that the chocolate cools.

Nutrition: 115 calories 7.3g fat 12.7g carbohydrates

219. Strawberry Angel Food Dessert

Preparation Time: 15 minutes
Cooking Time: 0 minute
Servings: 18

Ingredients
- angel cake (10 inches)
- packages of softened cream cheese
- 1 container (8 oz) of frozen fluff, thawed
- 1 liter of fresh strawberries, sliced
- 1 jar of strawberry icing

Direction
1. Crumble the cake in a 9 x 13-inch dish.
2. Beat the cream cheese and 1 cup sugar in a medium bowl until the mixture is light and fluffy. Stir in the whipped topping. Crush the cake with your hands, and spread the cream cheese mixture over the cake.
3. Combine the strawberries and the frosting in a bowl until the strawberries are well covered. Spread over the layer of cream cheese. Cool until ready to serve.

Nutrition: 261 calories 11g fat 3.2g protein

220. Key Lime Pie

Preparation Time: 8 minutes
Cooking Time: 9 minutes
Servings: 8

Ingredients
- (9-inch) prepared graham cracker crust
- cups of sweetened condensed milk
- 1/2 cup sour cream
- 3/4 cup lime juice
- 1 tablespoon grated lime zest

Direction
1. Preheat the oven to 175 ° C (350 ° F).
2. Combine the condensed milk, sour cream, lime juice, and lime zest in a medium bowl. Mix well and pour into the graham cracker crust.
3. Bake in the preheated oven for 5 to 8 minutes until small bubbles burst on the surface of the cake.

4. Cool the cake well before serving. Decorate with lime slices and whipped cream if desired.

Nutrition: 553 calories 20.5g fat 10.9g protein

221. Ice Cream Sandwich Dessert

Preparation Time: 20 minutes
Cooking Time: 0 minute
Servings: 12

Ingredients
- 22 ice cream sandwiches
- Frozen whipped topping in 16 oz container, thawed
- jar (12 oz) Caramel ice cream
- 1 1/2 cups of salted peanuts

Direction
1. Cut a sandwich in two. Place a whole sandwich and a half sandwich on a short side of a 9 x 13-inch baking dish. Repeat this until the bottom is covered, alternate the full sandwich, and the half sandwich.
2. Spread half of the whipped topping. Pour the caramel over it. Sprinkle with half the peanuts. Repeat the layers with the rest of the ice cream sandwiches, whipped cream, and peanuts.
3. Cover and freeze for up to 2 months. Remove from the freezer 20 minutes before serving. Cut into squares.

Nutrition: 559 calories 28.8g fat 10g protein

222. Bananas Foster

Preparation Time: 5 minutes
Cooking Time: 5 minutes
Servings: 4

Ingredients
- 2/3 cup dark brown sugar
- 1/2 teaspoons vanilla extract
- 1/2 teaspoon of ground cinnamon
- bananas, peeled and cut lengthwise and broad
- 1/4 cup chopped nuts, butter

Direction
1. Melt the butter in a deep-frying pan over medium heat. Stir in sugar, 3 ½ tbsp. of rum, vanilla, and cinnamon.
2. When the mixture starts to bubble, place the bananas and nuts in the pan. Bake until the bananas are hot, 1 to 2 minutes. Serve immediately with vanilla ice cream.

Nutrition: 534 calories 23.8g fat 4.6g protein

223. Rhubarb Strawberry Crunch

Preparation Time: 15 minutes
Cooking Time: 45 minutes
Servings: 18

Ingredients
- 3 tablespoons all-purpose flour
- 3 cups of fresh strawberries, sliced
- 3 cups of rhubarb, cut into cubes
- 1/2 cup flour
- 1 cup butter

Direction
1. Preheat the oven to 190 ° C.
2. Combine 1 cup of white sugar, 3 tablespoons flour, strawberries and rhubarb in a large bowl. Place the mixture in a 9 x 13-inch baking dish.
3. Mix 1 1/2 cups of flour, 1 cup of brown sugar, butter, and oats until a crumbly texture is obtained. You may want to use a blender for this. Crumble the mixture of rhubarb and strawberry.
4. Bake in the preheated oven for 45 minutes or until crispy and light brown.

Nutrition: 253 calories 10.8g fat 2.3g protein

224. Frosty Strawberry Dessert

Preparation Time: 5 minutes
Cooking Time: 21 minutes
Servings: 16

Ingredients
- cup flour, white sugar, whipped cream
- 1/2 cup chopped walnuts, butter
- cups of sliced strawberries
- tablespoons lemon juice
- 1/4 cup brown sugar

Direction
1. Preheat the oven to 175 ° C (350 ° F).
2. Mix the flour, brown sugar, nuts, and melted butter in a bowl. Spread on a baking sheet and bake for 20 minutes in the preheated oven until crispy. Remove from the oven and let cool completely.

3. Beat the egg whites to snow. Keep beating until you get firm spikes while slowly adding sugar. Mix the strawberries in the lemon juice and stir in the egg whites until the mixture turns slightly pink. Stir in the whipped cream until it is absorbed.
4. Crumble the walnut mixture and spread 2/3 evenly over the bottom of a 9-inch by 13-inch dish. Place the strawberry mixture on the crumbs and sprinkle the rest of the crumbs. Place in the freezer for two hours. Take them out of the freezer a few minutes before serving to facilitate cutting.

Nutrition: 184 calories 9.2g fat 2.2g protein

225. Dessert Pie

Preparation Time: 16 minutes
Cooking Time: 18 minutes
Servings: 12
Ingredients
- cup all-purpose flour
- 1 package of cream cheese
- 8 oz whipped cream topping
- 1 (4-oz) package of instant chocolate pudding
- 1/2 cup butter, white sugar

Direction
1. Preheat the oven to 175 ° C (350 ° F).
2. In a large bowl, mix butter, flour and 1/4 cup sugar until the mixture looks like coarse breadcrumbs. Push the mixture into the bottom of a 9 x 13-inch baking dish. Bake in the preheated oven for 15 to 18 minutes or until lightly browned to allow cooling to room temperature.
3. In a large bowl, beat cream cheese and 1/2 cup sugar until smooth. Stir in half of the whipped topping. Spread the mixture over the cooled crust.
4. Mix the pudding in the same bowl according to the instructions on the package. Spread over the cream cheese mixture.
5. Garnish with the remaining whipped cream. Cool in the fridge.

Nutrition: 376 calories 23g fat 3.6g protein

226. Sugar-Coated Pecans

Preparation Time: 15 minutes
Cooking Time: 1 hour
Servings: 12
Ingredients
- egg white
- 1 tablespoon water
- 1-pound pecan halves
- 1 cup white sugar
- 1/2 teaspoon ground cinnamon

Directions
1. Preheat the oven to 120 ° C (250 ° F). Grease a baking tray.
2. In a bowl, whisk the egg whites and water until frothy. Combine the sugar, ¾ tsp. salt, and cinnamon in another bowl.
3. Add the pecans to the egg whites and stir to cover the nuts. Remove the nuts and mix them with the sugar until well covered. Spread the nuts on the prepared baking sheet.
4. Bake for 1 hour at 250 ° F (120 ° C). Stir every 15 minutes.

Nutrition: 328 calories 27.2g fat 3.8g protein

227. Jalapeño Popper Spread

Preparation Time: 10 minutes
Cooking Time: 3 minutes
Servings: 32

Ingredients
- 2 packets of cream cheese, softened
- cup mayonnaise
- 1 (4-gram) can chopped green peppers, drained
- grams diced jalapeño peppers, canned, drained
- 1 cup grated Parmesan cheese

Direction
1. In a large bowl, mix cream cheese and mayonnaise until smooth. Stir the bell peppers and jalapeño peppers.
2. Pour the mixture into a microwave oven and sprinkle with Parmesan cheese.
3. Microwave on maximum power, about 3 minutes.

Nutrition: 110 calories 11.1g fat 2.1g protein

228. Brown Sugar Smokies

Preparation Time: 10 minutes
Cooking Time: 4 minutes
Servings: 12

Ingredients
- 1-pound bacon
- (16 ounces) package little smokie sausages
- 1 cup brown sugar, or to taste

Direction
1. Preheat the oven to 175 ° C (350 ° F).
2. Cut the bacon in three and wrap each strip around a little sausage. Place sausages wrapped on wooden skewers, several to one place the kebabs on a baking sheet and sprinkle generously with brown sugar.
3. Bake until the bacon is crispy, and the brown sugar has melted.

Nutrition: 356 calories 27.2g fat 9g protein

229. Fruit Dip

Preparation Time: 5 minutes
Cooking Time: 0 minute
Servings: 12

Ingredients
- (8-oz) package cream cheese, softened
- 1 (7-oz) jar marshmallow creme

Direction
1. Use an electric mixer to combine the cream cheese and marshmallow
2. Beat until everything is well mixed.

Nutrition: 118 calories 6.6g fat 13.4g carbohydrates

230. Banana & Tortilla Snacks

Preparation Time: 5 minutes
Cooking Time: 0 minute
Servings: 1

Ingredients
- flour tortilla (6 inches)
- tablespoons peanut butter
- 1 tablespoon honey
- 1 banana
- tablespoons raisins

Directions
1. Lay the tortilla flat. Spread peanut butter and honey on the tortilla. Place the banana in the middle and sprinkle the raisins. Wrap and serve.

Nutrition: 520 calories 19.3g fat 12.8g protein

231. Caramel Popcorn

Preparation Time: 30 minutes
Cooking Time: 1 hour
Servings: 20

Ingredients
- 2 cups brown sugar
- 1/2 cup of corn syrup
- 1/2 teaspoon baking powder
- teaspoon vanilla extract
- 5 cups of popcorn

Direction
1. Preheat the oven to 95° C (250° F). Put the popcorn in a large bowl.
2. Melt 1 cup of butter in a medium-sized pan over medium heat. Stir in brown sugar, 1 tsp. of salt, and corn syrup. Bring to a boil, constantly stirring — Cook without stirring for 4 minutes. Then remove from heat and stir in the soda and vanilla. Pour in a thin layer on the popcorn and stir well.
3. Place in two large shallow baking tins and bake in the preheated oven, stirring every 15 minutes for an hour. Remove from the oven and let cool completely before breaking into pieces.

Nutrition: 14g fat 253 calories 32.8g carbohydrates

232. Apple and Berries Ambrosia

Preparation Time: 15 minutes
Cooking Time: 0 minutes
Serves 4

Ingredients:
- 2 cups unsweetened coconut milk, chilled
- 2 tablespoons raw honey
- 1 apple, peeled, cored, and chopped
- 2 cups fresh raspberries
- 2 cups fresh blueberries

Direction
1. Spoon the chilled milk in a large bowl, then mix in the honey. Stir to mix well.
2. Then mix in the remaining ingredients. Stir to coat the fruits well and serve immediately.

Nutrition: 386 calories 21.1g fat 4.2g protein

233. Chocolate, Almond, and Cherry Clusters

Preparation Time: 15 minutes
Cooking Time: 3 minutes
Serving: 5

Ingredients:
- 1 cup dark chocolate (60% cocoa or higher), chopped
- 1 tablespoon coconut oil
- ½ cup dried cherries
- 1 cup roasted salted almonds

Direction
1. Line a baking sheet with parchment paper.
2. Melt the chocolate and coconut oil in a saucepan for 3 minutes. Stir constantly.
3. Turn off the heat and mix in the cherries and almonds.
4. Drop the mixture on the baking sheet with a spoon. Place the sheet in the refrigerator and chill for at least 1 hour or until firm.
5. Serve chilled.

Nutrition: 197 calories 13.2g fat 4.1g protein

234. Chocolate and Avocado Mousse

Preparation Time: 40 minutes
Cooking Time: 5 minutes
Serving: 5

Ingredients:
- 8 ounces (227 g) dark chocolate (60% cocoa or higher), chopped
- ¼ cup unsweetened coconut milk
- 2 tablespoons coconut oil
- 2 ripe avocados, deseeded
- ¼ cup raw honey

Direction:
1. Put the chocolate in a saucepan. Pour in the coconut milk and add the coconut oil.
2. Cook for 3 minutes or until the chocolate and coconut oil melt. Stir constantly.
3. Put the avocado in a food processor, then drizzle with honey and melted chocolate. Pulse to combine until smooth.
4. Pour the mixture in a serving bowl, then sprinkle with salt. Refrigerate to chill for 30 minutes and serve.

Nutrition: 654 calories 46.8g fat 7.2g protein

235. Coconut Blueberries with Brown Rice

Preparation Time: 55 minutes
Cooking Time: 10 minutes
Serving: 4

Ingredients:
- 1 cup fresh blueberries
- 2 cups unsweetened coconut milk
- 1 teaspoon ground ginger
- ¼ cup maple syrup
- 2 cups cooked brown rice

Direction
1. Put all the ingredients, except for the brown rice, in a pot. Stir to combine well.
2. Cook over medium-high heat for 7 minutes or until the blueberries are tender.
3. Pour in the brown rice and cook for 3 more minute or until the rice is soft. Stir constantly.
4. Serve immediately.

Nutrition: 470 calories 24.8g fat 6.2g protein

236. Glazed Pears with Hazelnuts

Preparation Time: 10 minutes
Cooking Time: 20 minutes
Serving: 4

Ingredients:
- 4 pears, peeled, cored, and quartered lengthwise
- 1 cup apple juice
- 1 tablespoon grated fresh ginger
- ½ cup pure maple syrup
- ¼ cup chopped hazelnuts

Direction
1. Put the pears in a pot, then pour in the apple juice. Bring to a boil over medium-high heat, then reduce the heat to medium-low. Stir constantly.
2. Cover and simmer for an additional 15 minutes or until the pears are tender.
3. Meanwhile, combine the ginger and maple syrup in a saucepan. Bring to a boil over medium-high heat. Stir frequently. Turn off the heat and transfer the syrup to a small bowl and let sit until ready to use.
4. Transfer the pears in a large serving bowl with a slotted spoon, then top the pears with syrup.
5. Spread the hazelnuts over the pears and serve immediately.

Nutrition: 287 calories 3.1g fat 2.2g protein

237. Lemony Blackberry Granita

Preparation Time: 10 minutes
Cooking Time: 0 minutes
Serving: 4

Ingredients:
- 1 pound (454 g) fresh blackberries
- 1 teaspoon chopped fresh thyme
- ¼ cup freshly squeezed lemon juice
- ½ cup raw honey
- ½ cup water

Direction
1. Put all the ingredients in a food processor, then pulse to purée.
2. Pour the mixture through a sieve into a baking dish. Discard the seeds that remain in the sieve.
3. Put the baking dish in the freezer for 2 hours. Remove the dish from the refrigerator and stir to break any frozen parts.
4. Return the dish back to the freezer for an hour, then stir to break any frozen parts again.
5. Return the dish to the freezer for 4 hours until the granita is completely frozen.
6. Remove it from the freezer and mash to serve.

Nutrition: 183 calories 1.1g fat 2.2g protein

238. Lemony Tea and Chia Pudding

Preparation Time: 30 minutes
Cooking Time: 0 minutes
Serving: 4

Ingredients:
- 2 teaspoons Matcha green tea powder (optional)
- 2 tablespoons ground chia seeds
- 1 to 2 dates
- 2 cups unsweetened coconut milk
- Zest and juice of 1 lime

Direction
1. Put all the ingredients in a food processor and pulse until creamy and smooth.
2. Pour the mixture in a bowl, then wrap in plastic. Store in the refrigerator for at least 20 minutes, then serve chilled.

Nutrition: 225 calories 20.1g fat 3.2g protein

239. Mint Banana Chocolate Sorbet

Preparation Time: 4 hours 5 minutes
Cooking Time: 0 minutes
Serves 1

Ingredients:
- 1 frozen banana
- 1 tablespoon almond butter
- 2 tablespoons minced fresh mint
- 2 to 3 tablespoons dark chocolate chips (60% cocoa or higher)
- 2 to 3 tablespoons goji (optional)

Direction
1. Put the banana, butter, and mint in a food processor. Pulse to purée until creamy and smooth.
2. Add the chocolate and goji, then pulse for several more times to combine well.
3. Pour the mixture in a bowl or a ramekin, then freeze for at least 4 hours before serving chilled.

Nutrition: 213 calories 9.8g fat 3.1g protein

240. Raspberry Yogurt Basted Cantaloupe

Preparation Time: 15 minutes
Cooking Time: 0 minutes
Serving: 6

Ingredients:
- 2 cups fresh raspberries, mashed
- 1 cup plain coconut yogurt
- ½ teaspoon vanilla extract
- 1 cantaloupe, peeled and sliced
- ½ cup toasted coconut flakes

Direction
1. Combine the mashed raspberries with yogurt and vanilla extract in a small bowl. Stir to mix well.
2. Place the cantaloupe slices on a platter, then top with raspberry mixture and spread with toasted coconut.
3. Serve immediately.

Nutrition: 75 calories 4.1g fat 1.2g protein

241. Simple Apple Compote

Preparation Time: 15 minutes
Cooking Time: 10 minutes
Serving: 4

Ingredients:
- 6 apples, peeled, cored, and chopped
- ¼ cup raw honey
- 1 teaspoon ground cinnamon
- ¼ cup apple juice

Direction
1. Put all the ingredients in a stockpot. Stir to mix well, then cook over medium-high heat for 10 minutes or until the apples are glazed by honey and lightly saucy. Stir constantly.
2. Serve immediately.

Nutrition: 246 calories 0.9g fat 1.2g protein

242. Simple Peanut Butter and Chocolate Balls

Preparation Time: 45 minutes
Cooking Time: 0 minutes
Serving: 15

Ingredients:
- ¾ cup creamy peanut butter
- ¼ cup unsweetened cocoa powder
- 2 tablespoons softened almond butter
- ½ teaspoon vanilla extract
- 1¾ cups maple sugar

Direction
1. Line a baking sheet with parchment paper.
2. Combine all the ingredients in a bowl. Stir to mix well.
3. Divide the mixture into 15 parts and shape each part into a 1-inch ball.
4. Arrange the balls on the baking sheet and refrigerate for at least 30 minutes, then serve chilled.

Nutrition: 146 calories 8.1g fat 4.2g protein

243. Simple Spiced Sweet Pecans

Preparation Time: 4 minutes
Cooking Time: 17 minutes
Serving: 4

Ingredients:
- 1 cup pecan halves
- 3 tablespoons almond butter
- 1 teaspoon ground cinnamon
- ½ teaspoon ground nutmeg
- ¼ cup raw honey

Direction
1. Preheat the oven to 350°F (180°C). Line a baking sheet with parchment paper.
2. Combine all the ingredients in a bowl. Stir to mix well, then spread the mixture in the single layer on the baking sheet with a spatula.
3. Bake in the preheated oven for 16 minutes or until the pecan halves are well browned.
4. Serve immediately.

Nutrition: 324 calories 29.8g fat 3.2g protein

244. Overnight Oats with Raspberries

Preparation Time: 5 minutes
Cooking Time: 0 minutes
Serving: 2

Ingredients:
- 2/3 cup unsweetened almond milk
- ¼ cup raspberries
- 1/3 cup rolled oats
- 1 teaspoon honey
- ¼ teaspoon turmeric

Direction
1. Place the almond milk, raspberries, rolled oats, honey, turmeric, 1/8 tsp. cinnamon, and a pinch of ground cloves in a mason jar. Cover and shake to combine.
2. Transfer to the refrigerator for at least 8 hours, preferably 24 hours.
3. Serve chilled.

Nutrition: 81 calories 1.9g fat 2.1g protein

246. Yogurt Sundae

Preparation Time: 5 minutes
Cooking Time: 0 minutes
Serving: 1

Ingredients:
- ¾ cup plain Greek yogurt
- ¼ cup fresh mixed berries (blueberries, strawberries, blackberries)
- 2 tablespoons walnut pieces
- 1 tablespoon ground flaxseed
- 2 fresh mint leaves, shredded

Direction
1. Pour the yogurt into a tall parfait glass and sprinkle with the mixed berries, walnut pieces, and flaxseed.
2. Garnish with the shredded mint leaves and serve immediately.

Nutrition: 236 calories 10.8g fat 21.1g protein

247. Blackberry-Yogurt Green

Preparation Time: 5 minutes
Cooking Time: 0 minutes
Serves 2

Ingredients:
- 1 cup plain Greek yogurt
- 1 cup baby spinach
- ½ cup frozen blackberries
- ½ cup unsweetened almond milk
- ¼ cup chopped pecans

Direction
1. Process the yogurt, baby spinach, blackberries, almond milk, and ½ tsp. ginger in a food processor until smoothly blended.
2. Divide the mixture into two bowls and serve topped with the chopped pecans.

Nutrition: 201 calories 14.5g fat 7.1g protein

248. Moroccan Stuffed Dates

Preparation Time: 16 minutes
Cooking Time: 0 minute
Serving: 30

Ingredients:
- 1 lb. dates
- 1 cup blanched almonds
- 1/4 cup sugar
- 1 1/2 tbsp orange flower water
- 1/4 teaspoon cinnamon

Directions:
1. Process the almonds, sugar and cinnamon in a food processor. Add 1 tbsp. butter and orange flower water and process until a smooth paste is formed.
2. Roll small pieces of almond paste the same length as a date. Take one date, make a vertical cut and discard the pit. Insert a piece of the almond paste and press the sides of the date firmly around. Repeat with all the remaining dates and almond paste.

Nutrition: 208 calories 12g fat 6g protein

249. Almond Cookies

Preparation Time: 13 minutes
Cooking Time: 10 minutes
Serving: 30

Ingredient:
- 1 cup almonds, blanched, toasted and finely chopped
- 1 cup powdered sugar
- 4 egg whites
- 2 tbsp flour
- 1/2 tsp vanilla extract

Directions:
1. Preheat oven to 320 F. Blend the almonds in a food processor until finely chopped.
2. Beat egg whites and sugar until thick. Add in vanilla extract and a pinch of cinnamon. Gently stir in almonds and flour. Place tablespoonfuls of mixture on two lined baking trays.
3. Bake for 10 minutes, or until firm. Turn oven off, leave the door open and leave cookies to cool. Dust with powdered sugar.

Nutrition: 219 calories 16g fat 8g protein

250. Watermelon Cream

Preparation Time: 15 minutes
Cooking Time: 0 minutes
Servings: 2

Ingredients:
- pound watermelon, peeled and chopped
- teaspoon vanilla extract
- 1 cup heavy cream
- 1 teaspoon lime juice
- tablespoons stevia

Directions:
1. In a blender, combine the watermelon with the cream and the rest of the ingredients, pulse well, divide into cups and keep in the fridge for 15 minutes before serving.

Nutrition: Calories 122 Fat 5.7 Fiber 3.2 Carbs 5.3 Protein 0.4

251. Grapes Stew

Preparation Time: 10 minutes
Cooking Time: 10 minutes
Servings: 4

Ingredients:
- 2/3 cup stevia
- tablespoon olive oil
- 1/3 cup coconut water
- teaspoon vanilla extract
- 1 teaspoon lemon zest, grated
- cup red grapes, halved

Directions:
1. Heat up a pan with the water over medium heat, add the oil, stevia and the rest of the ingredients, toss, simmer for 10 minutes, divide into cups and serve.

Nutrition: Calories 122 Fat 3.7 Fiber 1.2 Carbs 2.3 Protein 0.4

252. Cocoa Sweet Cherry Cream

Preparation Time: 2 hours
Cooking Time: 0 minutes
Servings: 4

Ingredients:
- ½ cup cocoa powder
- ¾ cup red cherry jam
- ¼ cup stevia
- 2 cups water
- pound cherries, pitted and halved

Directions:
In a blender, mix the cherries with the water and the rest of the ingredients, pulse well, divide into cups and keep in the fridge for 2 hours before serving.

Nutrition: Calories 162 Fat 3.4 Fiber 2.4 Carbs 5

253. Spanish Nougat

Preparation Time: 17 minutes
Cooking Time: 15 minutes
Serving: 24

Ingredients:
- 11/2 cup honey
- 3 egg whites
- 1 ¾ cup almonds, roasted and chopped

Directions:
1. Pour the honey into a saucepan and bring it to a boil over medium-high heat, then set aside to cool. Beat the egg whites to a thick glossy meringue and fold them into the honey.
2. Bring the mixture back to medium-high heat and let it simmer, constantly stirring, for 15 minutes. When the color and consistency change to dark caramel, remove from heat, add the almonds and mix trough.
3. Line a 9x13 inch pan with foil and pour the hot mixture on it. Cover with another piece of foil and even out. Let cool completely. Place a wooden board weighted down with some heavy cans on it. Leave like this for 3-4 days, so it hardens and dries out. Slice into 1-inch squares.

Nutrition: 189 calories 12g fat 5g protein

255. Cinnamon Butter Cookies

Preparation Time: 12 minutes
Cooking Time: 15 minutes
Serving: 24

Ingredients:
- 2 cups flour
- 1/2 cup sugar
- 5 tbsp butter
- 3 eggs
- 1 tbsp cinnamon

Directions:
1. Cream the butter and sugar until light and fluffy. Combine the flour and the cinnamon. Beat eggs into the butter mixture. Gently add in the flour. Turn the dough onto a lightly floured surface and knead just once or twice until smooth.
2. Form a roll and divide it into 24 pieces. Line baking sheets with parchment paper or grease them. Roll each piece of cookie dough into a long thin strip, then make a circle, flatten a little and set it on the prepared baking sheet. Bake cookies, in batches, in a preheated to 350 F oven, for 12 to 15 minutes. Set aside to cool on a cooling rack.

Nutrition: 199 calories 13g fat 4g protein

256. Best French Meringues

Preparation Time: 15 minutes
Cooking Time: 2 hours
Serving: 36

Ingredients:
- 4 egg whites
- 2 1/4 cups powdered sugar

Directions:
1. Preheat the oven to 200 F. and line a baking sheet.
2. In a glass bowl, beat egg whites with an electric mixer. Add in sugar a little at a time, while continuing to beat at medium speed. When the egg white mixture becomes stiff and shiny like satin, transfer to a large pastry bag. Pipe the meringue onto the lined baking sheet with the use of a large star tip.
3. Place the meringues in the oven and leave the oven door slightly ajar. Bake for 2 1/2 hours, or until the meringues are dry, and can easily be removed from the pan.

Nutrition: 210 calories 16g fat 9g protein

257. Cinnamon Palmiers

Preparation Time: 9 minutes
Cooking Time: 17 minutes
Serving: 30

Ingredients:
- 1/3 cup granulated sugar
- 2 tsp cinnamon
- 1/2 lb. puff pastry
- 1 egg, beaten (optional)

Directions:
1. Stir together the sugar and cinnamon. Roll the pastry dough into a large rectangle. Spread the cinnamon sugar in an even layer over the dough.
2. Starting at the long ends of the rectangle, loosely roll each side inward until they meet in the middle. If needed, brush it with the egg to hold it together.
3. Slice the pastry roll crosswise into 1/4-inch pieces and arrange them on a lined with parchment paper baking sheet. Bake cookies in a preheated to 400 F oven for 12-15 minutes, until they puff and turn golden brown. Serve warm or at room temperature.

Nutrition: 211 calories 17g fat 6g protein

258. Baked Apples

Preparation Time: 17 minutes
Cooking Time: 10 minutes
Serving: 4

Ingredients:
- 8 medium sized apples
- 1/3 cup walnuts, crushed
- 3/4 cup sugar
- 3 tbsp raisins, soaked in brandy or dark rum
- 2 oz butter

Directions:
1. Peel and carefully hollow the apples. Prepare stuffing by beating the butter, 3/4 cup of sugar, crushed walnuts, raisins and cinnamon.
2. Stuff the apples with this mixture and place them in an oiled dish. Sprinkle the apples with 1-2 tablespoons of water and bake in a moderate oven. Serve warm with a scoop of vanilla ice cream.

Nutrition: 219 calories 12g fat 5g protein

259. Pumpkin Baked with Dry Fruit

Preparation Time: 18 minutes
Cooking Time: 15 minutes
Serving: 6

Ingredients:
- lb. pumpkin, cut into medium pieces
- 1 cup dry fruit (apricots, plums, apples, raisins)
- 1/2 cup brown sugar

Directions:
1. Soak the dry fruit in some water, drain and discard the water. Cut the pumpkin in medium cubes. At the bottom of a pot arrange a layer of pumpkin pieces, then a layer of dry fruit and then again, some pumpkin.
2. Add a little water. Cover the pot and bring to boil. Simmer until there is no more water left. When almost ready add the sugar. Serve warm or cold.

Nutrition: 200 calories 14g fat 7g protein

260. Quick Peach Tarts

Preparation Time: 14 minutes
Cooking Time: 10 minutes
Serving: 4

Ingredients:
- 1 sheet frozen ready-rolled puff pastry
- 1/4 cup light cream cheese spread
- 2 tablespoons sugar
- a pinch of cinnamon
- 4 peaches, peeled, halved, stones removed, sliced

Directions:
1. Line a baking tray with baking paper. Cut the pastry into 4 squares and place them on the prepared tray. Using a spoon, mix cream cheese, sugar, vanilla and cinnamon. Spread over pastry squares. Arrange peach slices on top.
2. Bake in a preheated to 350 F oven for 10 minutes, or until golden.

Nutrition: 205 calories 13g fat 4g protein

261. Bulgarian Rice Pudding

Preparation Time: 8 minutes
Cooking Time: 15 minutes
Serving 4-5

Ingredients:
- 1 cup short-grain white rice
- 6 tbsp sugar
- 1 1/2 cup whole milk, water
- 1 cinnamon stick
- 1 strip lemon zest

Directions:
1. Place the rice in a saucepan, cover with water and cook over low heat for about 15 minutes. Add milk, sugar, a cinnamon stick and lemon zest and cook over very low heat, stirring frequently, until the mixture is creamy. Do not let it boil. When ready, discard the cinnamon stick and lemon zest. Serve warm or at room temperature.

Nutrition: 187 calories 10g fat 3g protein

262. Caramel Cream

Preparation Time: 18 minutes
Cooking Time: 1 hour
Serving: 8

Ingredients:
- 11/2 cup sugar
- 4 cups cold milk
- 8 eggs
- 2 tsp vanilla powder

Directions:
1. Melt 1/4 of the sugar in a non-stick pan over low heat. When the sugar has turned into caramel, pour it into 8 cup-sized ovenproof pots covering only the bottoms.
2. Whisk the eggs with the rest of the sugar and the vanilla, and slowly add the milk. Stir the mixture well and divide between the pots.
3. Place the 8 pots in a larger, deep baking dish. Pour 3-4 cups of water into the dish. Place the baking dish in a preheated to 280 F oven for about an hour and bake but do not let the water boil, as the boiling will overcook the cream and make holes in it: if necessary, add cold water to the baking dish.
4. Remove the baking dish from the oven; remove the pots from the dish. Place a shallow serving plate on top, then invert each pot so that the cream unmolds. The caramel will form a topping and sauce.

Nutrition: 213 calories 16g fat 8g protein

263. Yogurt-Strawberries Ice Pops

Preparation Time: 4 hours
Cooking Time: 0 minute
Serving: 8-9

Ingredients:
- 3 cups yogurt
- 3 tbsp honey
- 2 cups strawberries, quartered

Direction
1. Strain the yogurt in a clean white dishtowel. Combine the strained yogurt with honey.
2. Blend the strawberries with a blender then gently fold the strawberry puree into the yogurt mixture until just barely combined, with streaks remaining. Divide evenly among the molds, insert the sticks and freeze for 3 to 4 hours until solid.

Nutrition: 216 calories 16g fat 8g protein

264. Fresh Strawberries in Mascarpone and Rose Water

Preparation Time: 11 minutes
Cooking Time: 0 minute
Serving: 4

Ingredients:
- 6 oz strawberries, washed
- 1 cup mascarpone cheese
- 1/2 teaspoon rose water
- 1/2 teaspoon vanilla extract
- 1/4 cup white sugar

Directions:
1. In a bowl, combine together the mascarpone cheese, sugar, rose water and vanilla. Divide the strawberries into 4 dessert bowls. Add two dollops of mascarpone mixture on top and serve.

Nutrition: 197 calories 10g fat 3g protein

265. Delicious French Eclairs

Preparation Time: 23 minutes
Cooking Time: 43 minutes
Serving: 12

Ingredients:
- 1/2 cup butter
- 1 cup boiling water
- 1 cup sifted flour
- 4 eggs
- a pinch of salt

Directions:
1. In a medium saucepan, combine butter, salt, and boiling water. Bring to the boil, then reduce heat and add a cup of flour all at once, stirring vigorously until mixture forms a ball.
2. Remove from heat and add eggs, one at a time, whisking well to incorporate completely after each addition. Continue beating until the mixture is thick and shiny and breaks from the spoon.
3. Pipe or spoon onto a lined baking sheet then bake for 20 minutes in a preheated to 450 F oven. Reduce heat to 350 F and bake for 20 minutes more, or until golden. Set aside to cool and fill with sweetened whipped cream or custard.

Nutrition: 220 calories 17g fat 5g protein

266. Blueberry Yogurt Dessert

Preparation Time: 18 minutes
Cooking Time: 0 minute
Serving: 6

Ingredients:
- 1/3 cup blueberry jam
- 1 cup fresh blueberries
- 2 tbsp powdered sugar
- 1 cup heavy cream
- 2 cups yogurt

Directions:
1. Strain the yogurt in a piece of cheesecloth.
2. In a large bowl, beat the cream and powdered sugar until soft peaks form. Add strained yogurt and 1 tsp. of vanilla and beat until medium peaks form and the mixture is creamy and thick.
3. Gently fold half the fresh blueberries and the blueberry jam into cream mixture until just

barely combined, with streaks remaining. Divide dessert among 6 glass bowls, top with fresh blueberries and serve.

Nutrition: 208 calories 12g fat 6g protein

WEEK 1 MEAL PLAN

DAY	BREAKFAST	MAIN DISH	SIDES	DESSERT
SUNDAY	Egg with Zucchini Noodles	Steak with Olives and Mushroom	Lemon Fruit and Nut Bars	Chocolate Ganache
MONDAY	Banana Oats	Spicy Mustard Chicken	Cauliflower Fried Rice with Bacon	Chocolate Covered Strawberries
TUESDAY	Berry Oats	Walnut and Oregano Crusted Chicken	White Lasagna Stuffed Peppers	Strawberry Angel Food Dessert
WEDNESDAY	Sun-Dried Tomatoes Oatmeal	Chicken and Onion Casserole	Boiled Eggs with Butter and Thyme	Key Lime Pie
THURSDAY	Quinoa Muffins	Chicken and Mushroom	Fluffy Microwave Scrambled Eggs	Ice Cream Sandwich Dessert
FRIDAY	Watermelon Pizza	Herb-Roasted Lamb Leg	Caesar Salad Deviled Eggs	Bananas Foster
SATURDAY	Cheesy Yogurt	Spring Lamb Stew	Sour Cream and Chive Egg Clouds	Dessert Pie

WEEK 2 MEAL PLAN

DAY	BREAKFAST	MAIN DISH	SIDES	DESSERT
SUNDAY	Avocado and Chickpea Sandwiches	Baked-Lemon-Butter Fish	Pistachio Arugula Salad	Apple and Berries Ambrosia
MONDAY	Raisin Quinoa Breakfast	Fish Taco Bowl	Potato Salad	Chocolate, Almond, and Cherry Clusters
TUESDAY	Banana Cinnamon Fritters	Scallops with Creamy Bacon Sauce	Flavorful Braised Kale	Chocolate and Avocado Mousse
WEDNESDAY	Okra and Tomato Casserole	Shrimp and Avocado Lettuce Cups	Bean Salad	Coconut Blueberries with Brown Rice
THURSDAY	Ground Beef and Brussels Sprouts	Garlic Butter Shrimp	Basil Tomato Skewers	Glazed Pears with Hazelnuts
FRIDAY	Italian Mini Meatballs	Pork Rind Salmon Cakes	Olives with Feta	Lemony Blackberries Granita
SATURDAY	Salmon Kebabs	Creamy Dill Salmon	Black Bean Medley	Mint Banana Chocolate Sorbet

CONCLUSION

Changing your eating habits to follow the Mediterranean diet can be very exciting. Knowing that you're making the conscious decision to improve your diet – and your life – in a positive way and eating healthier is the first step of the Mediterranean diet. It might seem overwhelming at first, but you don't have to make all the changes in one day. The smaller changes you make, the more benefits you'll see, which will inspire you to make more beneficial changes. Those benefits will pay off big in the long run – for you and your family.

To successfully incorporate this new way of eating into your life, you should seriously consider adopting other parts of the Mediterranean lifestyle as well.

The Mediterranean diet – a well-balanced diet that includes healthy fats and complex carbohydrates – offers the best alternative to popular fad diets if you're looking to lose weight without sacrificing your health. By pairing this eating plan with lower stress and increased exercise, you can do more than just lose a few pounds; you can also reduce your blood pressure, cholesterol, and blood sugar.

One of the important influences' diets can have upon health is by merely establishing weight control. Being overweight can damage every body system and risk all our most serious, debilitating diseases. The Mediterranean diet helps one maintain a healthy weight by providing complex carbohydrates, fiber, and protein to help you feel full and slow digestion, so you feel satisfied.

One of the most critical keys to revamping your lifestyle to fit your new eating habits is stress reduction! This instruction may be a tricky one; after all, we all have periods of stress in our lives. Additionally, some of us seem destined to have more pressure in our lives than other people. Regardless, handling stress should begin with finding a realistic perspective on the factors that cause our stress and then doing what we can to change those factors. Maybe you can't follow the Mediterranean habit of taking a 2-hour midday break, but you can incorporate ways to reduce your stress throughout your day.

In the fast-paced and highly technical era we live in, it's sometimes hard to make time for your family. However, it should be a priority. Try planning dinner times so everyone can sit and eat a meal together. It helps build relationships and connections. Much research has shown that people with strong family interaction are less likely to suffer from depression.

If you don't live near any family members, you can create the same atmosphere with friends. Try planning weekly or bi-weekly get-togethers and maybe having a different friend host it each time. Making meals potlucks takes the stress off any one person preparing a big meal. When you go, take a Mediterranean diet recipe to share with your friends!

Besides reducing your stress level, getting more daily physical activity, and increasing your family time are solid guidelines that you should consider beginning to incorporate into your new way of life. Remember, no one is expecting you to make dramatic changes overnight.

www.ingramcontent.com/pod-product-compliance
Ingram Content Group UK Ltd.
Pitfield, Milton Keynes, MK11 3LW, UK
UKHW050416240426
12048UKWH00021B/1547